V O I C E S *of*
QUEDGELEY
AND HARDWICKE

Snow on the tow path looking from Hardwicke Bridge House towards Sharpness.

VOICES *of*
QUEDGELEY
AND HARDWICKE

S A N D R A   A S H E N F O R D

Front cover illustration (above): The crew of a dredger on the Gloucester Sharpness canal. Contributor John Drinkwater's father is one of the men.

Dedication

For my family; past, present and future

First published 2002
Reprinted 2003

Reprinted in 2014 by
The Histoy Press
The Mill, Brimscombe Port,
Stroud, Gloucestershire, GL5 2QG
www.thehistorypress.co.uk

British Library Cataloguing in Publication Data.
A catalogue record for this book is available from the British Library.

ISBN 978 0 7524 2655 6

Printed and bound in Great Britain by
Marston Book Services Ltd, Oxfordshire

Contents

Introduction   7

Acknowledgements   8

1. A Country Childhood   9

2. Family Life   18

3. Shops and Trades   30

4. Around the Villages   47

5. Hardwicke Reformatory   60

6. On the Canal   64

7. During the War   76

8. Leisure Time and Celebration   80

9. Down on the Farm   97

10. Times of Change   116

Charlie Smith, whose recollections are included in this book, pictured with his prize at the annual Hardwicke Fruit, Flower and Vegetable Show in 1969.

Introduction

It was on a sunny, summer's day nine years ago that I first set eyes on the former bridgekeeper's cottage in Hardwicke that was to become my home. I didn't want to move to the area – 'it's just a big housing estate,' I moaned to my husband Matt, when he first suggested it. How wrong I was. Hardwicke has a lot of new housing, but at its core it is still a predominantly rural community, with church and school and pubs as the focus of village life. Quedgeley is just the same – a village heart beating in the midst of massive new development.

But as I began writing this book, I realised that there was a real danger that the histories of these two communities were disappearing along with the green fields and native trees. Real characters such as Charlie Smith, Vic Charles, the village postman and Tom Fredericks, the Hardwicke bridgeman, have all passed away and key landmarks, like the Hardwicke Reformatory, have been demolished. Hardwicke Bridge House, once the domain of the legendary Mr Fredericks and now home to the Ashenford family, was a derelict wreck, in spite of its listed status, and it took a huge amount of faith and commitment to bring it back to life and so save another little piece of history.

But does it matter? Does it matter if no-one knows that Quedgeley and Hardwicke were once separate villages with their own distinct characters, rather than one big suburb of Gloucester, with its associated problems of vandalism and joy-riding? I think it does, and it has been a huge privilege to talk to the contributors to this book and share their memories of a quieter, perhaps more contented time. Life in the villages was hard, but everyone knew everyone else and neighbours could be relied on in a crisis. It is perhaps strange to think now of a village up in arms against the introduction of street lights, but no-one had any fear of crime and children would walk around the dark lanes without giving their parents cause for concern.

But not all progress was unwelcome – the introduction of mains water in the 1950s was remembered as quite something and, after years of going down the garden to use the loo, or drawing water from the well for washday, running water was quite a novelty!

Now when I travel around the villages, it is fascinating to pick out the properties that were once a shop, or a workshop and to see how old and new have blended in together. We can't stop the 'progress', and it would be pointless to try to 'preserve' the villages; they are a living entity and will continue to change, sometimes for the better and sometimes not.

The aim of this book, then, has not been to record history in the usual sense of the word – it is not a record of important dates and events. Rather it is a chat with some of the people who, like all of us who live or work here, have contributed to making Quedgeley and Hardwicke the communities that they are today. After all, our lives are tomorrow's history.

Sandra Ashenford
Hardwicke
Gloucester

Acknowledgements

My heartfelt thanks go to everyone listed in this book who gave their time and memories so freely and generously, and their precious photographs, when I asked for help. I hope I have captured some of the flavour of these wonderful stories and I hope the contributors will forgive any unintended inaccuracies on my part.

Special thanks to John Roche and John and Eileen Bell who came up trumps in response to my last-minute panic call for extra photographs and also to Charles and Sally Lloyd-Baker for lending me the picture of Miss Olive Lloyd-Baker.

In addition, my thanks go to Dave Bailes, not only for his own contributions to this book, but also for carrying out some of the interviews and for putting at my disposal the files of the Hardwicke Historical Society. These included the memories of the late Charlie Smith, one of the great village 'characters'. Charlie's recollections, not only of his own early life, but also the lives of his father, grandfather and great grandfather would have been lost had it not been for the local historians who had the foresight to capture his words for posterity. My thanks also to Charlie's family for allowing his memories to be used in this book and for lending me the pictures of St Crispin's.

Some other memories included here were also originally gathered by the Historical Society and were first published in the village magazine *Hardwicke Matters*. Richard Cale's wonderful stories about his father and grandfather and his own childhood in Quedgeley were first published in *Quedgeley News*, the magazine for that village. Both publications work hard to help ensure 'community spirit' lives on in these villages.

Special thanks also go to Margaret Tuckwell for the fascinating memories of her father, the village postman. Margaret has also researched and written a detailed history of the Hardwicke Reformatory which I would recommend to anyone who wants to find out more about this piece of national social history.

Finally, I have to say a big thank-you to my husband Matt and daughters Morgan, Portia and Perdita for their contributions included here, and especially for their support, patience and endless cups of tea as deadline loomed and panic set in.

And to my friend, Katie Jarvis, who wrote *Minchinhampton and Nailsworth Voices*, and so inspired this volume.

1 A Country Childhood

Small schools

Hardwicke School was where the fencing place is now, opposite Hardwicke church. It had two rooms and bucket toilets. The teachers lived in Naas Lane, in a bungalow. Quedgeley School was also small. A bigger school was built where the St James Centre is now.

Bettina Brewis
(b. 1922)

A strict headteacher

Miss Stephens was the headteacher there when I was at Hardwicke school. We were really frightened to death of her, she was so strict. I had the cane many a time for being a bad boy! It was only natural. If you were naughty you had the cane. But they only caned you on the one hand, the left hand if you were right handed, they didn't cane you on the hand you wrote with! But it didn't make thugs out of us - it did us good. It was Miss Stephens who administered the cane.

There was one big classroom, which had the seniors at one end and the juniors at the other, and the little classroom was for the infants. And then the cloakroom was on the side. To heat the school they had one of those big old, tall combustion stoves. We filled it up with coke and all that, that's all we had in them days.

We took our own sandwiches for lunch and we used to pay a ha'penny, or a penny, for a mug of Horlicks. We would play old fashioned games, and we played football. We used to play out in the playground, skipping or rounders and things like that. We had a concert nearly every year, and we used to dress up, the Lloyd-Bakers used to dress us up. We used to have to go to their house. The one particular house we used to go to was called The Cottage, opposite where the Village Hall and the Legion is now, a big house there. We used to go there and try on all these fancy dress clothes and all that, to have on the stage.

If you managed, I think it was, four or five years attendance without being late or absent you used to get medals, and after five or six years you had a watch. My sister had two or three medals.

Ivor Prosser
(b. 1919)

A reluctant pupil

My earliest memory is my first day at school – I cried all day. I didn't like it one little bit – I had been used to running wild. But I got to love it. We had a good headmistress in Miss Stephens. There were two rooms at Hardwicke school, the infants were in the small room and then there was one long room. One teacher taught at one end, and the other taught at the other end but you always used to listen to the other teacher. I suppose it was very difficult! I left Hardwicke school when I was eleven. I'd won a free place to Sir Thomas Riches, and the Education Committee bought me a bicycle,

Pupils at Hardwicke school in 1927.

because there were no buses. I had a brand new bicycle and I got to school all right. We did a five and a half days a week and we played football on the Wednesday afternoons.

John Drinkwater
(b. 1915)

Dirty feet

School in my day was quite different to what it is now because the lane was filthy dirty and Hardwicke school was close to a farm, with dirt all over the road. In those days there was no school kitchen. Children brought their own food – bread and cheese or bread and jam, and a bottle of cold tea. The plot of grass opposite the school was where we played football. The children in those days had to walk to school, some coming from Grove End and Moreton Valence. In winter we gave concerts and the school would be packed with parents and friends. This was followed by prize giving and medals for good attendance.

The boys played football on the piece of land opposite the school in winter and it became waterlogged and filthy dirty. They then used to come back into school so there was dirt all over the floor. It was dreadful and I've seen them sweep the school out with a hard bass broom to get rid of some of the dirt. The headmistress, Miss Stephens, was a terrible person, a good schoolteacher, but very hot tempered and in those days she was very, very, liberal with the cane. You had to come out in front and stand and have three on each hand. I don't know what parents would think if their children were served like that today.

Charlie Smith

A free ride

Mr Townsend was a commercial traveller. He used to have a car with running boards on the side. He had two children, a boy and a girl, and he used to take them to Hardwicke School each morning before he went to work and he used to let us stragglers stand on the running board – we weren't allowed inside – we used to stand on the running board and go to school.

John Drinkwater

Allotment manure

We had bucket toilets at Hardwicke school and a man in the village used to come up in the evenings and get the buckets from our toilets. He would put one on each of the handlebars of his bike and take them and put them on the allotments, just up Pound Lane - and that's how he used to grow such good vegetables!

Eric Perkins
(b. 1934)

Sweets before school

We had one shop, opposite the Old Hall in Hardwicke, called The Red House. Mrs Margaret owned that. We used to spend our pennies there and have our sweets there on the way to school. There was also another little shop just nearly opposite the Morning Star, which belonged to Mrs Stevens. In those days Hardwicke Post Office was where Elmlea is, just by Buckles Pool, by the pond. And it shifted then farther up into Sellars Road, to a

Hardwicke school pupils in 1930, including contributor Evelyn Sims (n–e Wyer) with her sisters Doris, who died at the age of twenty-three of Tuberculosis, and Yvonne, who emigrated to Canada in 1947 with a Canadian airman. Norman Sims, Evelyn's husband, is in the back row.

Mrs Pittaway in a house called Westbourne, she had it for years and years. It was there for a few years, then eventually it moved down to another house called Llanwern, still in Sellars Road. That was the last place I know of until it eventually packed up and went into Springfield.

Ivor Prosser
(b. 1919)

Fruit thieves

There was an old farmer at Church Farm, Mr Cousins, and in the season when the fruit was out in the orchard opposite the school the boys used to get out there after the fruit. The old man used to come down to the school and hammer on the front door with his stick and our teacher, Miss Stephens, used to go out to him. 'Well, what's the matter Mr Cousins?' she would ask. 'Them boys been after the fruit again!' he would shout. He'd come in and vow vengeance on the children and he'd threaten with his stick what he'd do to them. Oh, he was a terrible man like that and he tried to frighten them, but it didn't have any effect, they were out there again the next day.

Charlie Smith

Staying in line

There was the local school where you went from five to ten or eleven. The school building is now Hardy's Fencing. It was two rooms, one big one which was divided with the seniors at one end and the juniors at the other, and another room at the back for the infants. There was this big tortoise stove which you shovelled the coke in – that was the only heating it had, and of course we had to go outside to the toilets. Miss Stephens was the headmistress and she lived in a little cottage

at the top of Pound Lane which is still there now. She used to come down, a very tall lady with grey hair, her suitcase in her right hand. She used to stride down there – we were very scared of her – you didn't step out of line with Miss Stephens.

Evelyn Sims
(b. 1923)

Off with the hounds

In the winter the hounds met at Hardwicke Court fairly frequently, and on these days, during playtime, some of the boys were always missing - they would go off hunting! The headmistress would miss them and send a boy off to find them. He would go off and forget to come back, so she lost another!

Charlie Smith

A ticklish time!

Little thing always amused us - because there was no water laid on there at Hardwicke school, no sanitary and all that, and we used to have a big water churn thing, on wheels. We used to push that across to where Mrs Coule lived by the church, fill up with water there and then back across to school. That's how we had our water.

The toilets had buckets in, the boys' backing onto the girls' toilets. The man who cleared the buckets had to reach through a little door to get them from the girls' side. We used to open this door a bit when the girls were in there and tickle their bottoms with a nettle! They always threatened to tell on us but never did.

Ivor Prosser
(b. 1919)

Bettina Brewis with her daughter Diane on the playing field at Quedgeley, around 1945.

Getting about

When we were in our teens, basically if you wanted to go to a dance at Whitminster or Frampton or somewhere, you cycled. When I passed the exam to go to Ribston, you could either have your pass fare paid all the time you were at school or they would give you a bicycle, which you could keep afterwards. So I, and many others, opted for the bicycles and I kept that bicycle for years after I left school.

Evelyn Sims
(b. 1923)

The school run

In the same year Evelyn went to Ribston, three of us - myself, Ken Randall and Maurice Mitchell - we went to Stroud Central School and we used to cycle. We used to leave here at about half past seven in the morning and cycle to Stonehouse, put our bicycles in the stone house of the schools' inspector - Miss

Stephens, our teacher arranged for us to leave our bicycles there - and then we would catch the little train, the Dudbridge Donkey, and that went to a halt, a little station by the school. But after about eighteen months we didn't bother, and we cycled all the way into Stroud. And on a Saturday, Ken Randall and I, who would be playing football for the school, we would think nothing of cycling from here to Rodborough, Minchinhampton or Thrupp, or Brimscombe and come back in the afternoon and play for Hardwicke.

Norman Sims
(b. 1921)

Sweet labour

When I was ten I went to King's school at Gloucester. I used to catch the bus in every day basically because a lot of Denmark Road and Ribston Hall girls caught the same bus so I got them trained to do my homework for me in exchange for some sweet coupons.

Eric Vick

Diane Brewis with her bicycle and special doll in Quedgeley.

Skating on the pond

Where Hardwicke Court dairy is now there used to be a big orchard and in the middle was a big, big pond and when that used to freeze over we used to go on there ice-skating. Sometimes we would even try to ride bikes across it. There were a lot of ponds about – there's still one in Pound Lane now. There used to be another big one just in front of the house by the church, and another one at the back of the school.

Eric Perkins
(b. 1934)

Quedgeley Scouts

I was fortunate to grow up in Quedgeley when it was a small, rural, roadside village – although my parents and grandparents could remember a Quedgeley far more rural still. Entertainment was often scarce, however, so when the Quedgeley Scouts group was started by Bill Cottral, I was one of the first to join. We held our first meetings by the old rectory in Quedgeley's very first old school, now demolished, which was built by the Curtis Hayward family. I well remember one camp we organised at Edale in the Peak District when we were washed out and spent the rest of the camp billeted in the farmer's barn! Then at a later date on another camp, Mr Parker, our Senior Scout Leader, took us to Belgium and Luxembourg. We camped in a chalet, which seemed fine except we were all bitten by fleas the first night! The following day we had to throw all the bedding out which seemed to solve the problem. Quedgeley's first wooden Scout hut, which I helped to erect, came from Northleach prison, now a museum. This was followed by the modern building we have today, which was opened by the late Princess Margaret in 1988.

Richard Cale
(b. 1943)

Sheep shearing

As a boy I spent my spare time with the farmer next door, Mr Percy Davis, I more-or-less lived there with him on the farm. His house was actually joined onto us at Springfield and I lived on his farm with him practically every day. I used to go around mowing and all that. My father used to shear sheep, we used to go up to Colethrop Farm after school and it was our job to turn the wheel for the shearing machine. Well, this is a true story, our dad was shearing these sheep and this tramp came along, hair down to his shoulders. Our dad says: 'Looks like you could do with a damned hair cut, and the chap said: 'Ar'. So our dad sat him on a stool and sheared this bloke the whole way over. 'You come back again next year and I'll give you another one!', Dad said.

Ivor Prosser
(b. 1919)

Hardwicke school, 1931/32.

Sleepy Hollow

My friend Christine lived in a little lane off Naas Lane. She lived right down the bottom – there were no lights or anything like that. It was known as Sleepy Hollow. It was as dark as dark down there, and yet I never had any fear of walking down there. You never used to hear of people being attacked in those days, and mum never used to worry about me going down to see Christine in the dark. I always felt perfectly safe. There was a beautiful little wood there, full of bluebells. It's still there. A little gang of us often used to go down there and play.

Valerie Hodges
(b. 1943)

Muddy shoes

We were living at Grove End and we used to walk down the ballast to Hardwicke school, through about two or three inches of mud where the cattle had cut it all about. We used to come down three times on a Sunday – in the morning for choir, Sunday school in the afternoon and then Evensong. And every time we had to clean our shoes.

Norman Sims
(b. 1921)

Pulling the levers

In the 70s, when we used to cycle up that way, Mr Gray, the signalman, used to let my brother Gary and I pull the levers at the level crossing in Naas Lane. It took two of us to do it. He had his little house opposite the signal box, and he used to grow all his plants on the steps of the signal box. His daughters were Pat and Jane Gray.

Richard Hodges
(b. 1971)

Hardwicke school, 1933/34.

A painful lesson

When Hardwicke Bridge was there, we used to go up what we called the ballast and practice riding bikes. I learned to ride my first bike up the ballast. They were 'rat-trap' pedals with spikes on the end – I've still got the scar on my leg from where I slipped.

Eric Perkins
(b. 1934)

Collecting conkers

Where Tesco is now there used to be a cornfield, and there were a lot of conker trees. We used to park our bikes there and we would have to trample over three or four fields just to get to this side of the canal to do a spot of fishing. We used to go conkering down there too.

Richard Hodges
(b. 1971)

The policeman's parcel

As youngsters we used to make a parcel up and put a long bit of string on it. We would put the parcel down in the road and hide. They would come out of the Morning Star and we would pull the string so the parcel moved away. We did it once to the local policeman – we scampered away the first time, but he got wise to us and followed the string!

Norman Sims

The nicest people

Elmgrove Road East was a very dark road to walk down, pitch black as street lights were unheard of in Hardwicke at that time. Mr Davis liked potato peelings and scraps of food for his cattle and pigs. We used to load up two or three buckets of peelings, stale bread and leftovers each week, and if it was a good load we would get a thr'penny bit. If we only had half a bucket, or he wasn't in the best of moods, we would only get one old penny. With an old big penny you could buy four big gobstoppers or three sugar shrimps. With a thr'penny piece you could buy a lucky bag, or enough sweets to last you all the week. We used to wait at the door whilst Mr Davis found us some money and Mrs Davis would shout at us to come inside and sit by the fire with her. She always had something for us, whether it was an apple, cake or a bar of chocolate. Mr and Mrs Davis were the nicest of people and will always be a part of Hardwicke. I remember the counter in the Davis' shop being very high and having to jump up to put my money on it. You never used to see who was serving you, you just saw a big hand come over the counter. Across the road – where Hardwicke Newsmarket now stands – was the rival shop of Mr and Mrs Vallender, who had one son, Nicholas, which was also the post office. The Vallenders also had a shop on the Bristol Road, opposite Green lane, before they came into Elmgrove Road East. Mr Vallender had a smallholding at the back where he kept a lot of hens and chickens. The small holding had black pitch covered sheds, a barn full of hay and straw for Nicholas' horse and deep littered hen houses with open fields behind them running down to Dimore brook. Hildyard Close occupies the land now.

Mary Sims

Margaret Tuckwell (née Charles) and her brother Owen in 1963 in the front garden at Parklands when the fields opposite belonged to Field Court Farm, now a housing estate.

2 Family Life

The Sims family, returning from a rummage sale at Hardwicke school, at Cooles Corner in 1926/27.

A difficult birth

It was 1941 and they wouldn't let me have my baby at home because we didn't have water. So I had to go into my sister's in town to have the baby. You couldn't get into hospital if you had a house. It was scary. I started on the Friday night but I didn't have him until the Sunday. I had a little nurse who was learning. It was snowing and my husband had to go and fetch her from Clarence Street – all the nurses were in Clarence Street. She was learning to ride a bike, and she kept falling off this bike in the snow. My husband had to keep putting her back on the bike. And we had this tiny little fireplace in the bedroom with about two pieces of coal on and she was sat down knitting these navy blue ankle socks. I said to her: 'Can't you do something?' and she said, 'You wanted this baby, you'll just have to put up with it!' Eventually I had my son, Kenneth.

Marjorie Dobbs
(b. 1916)

A harsh upbringing

I was born in the village of New Marske, near Redcar in Yorkshire. I was a baby when my father died and my mother died when I was seven. She had wanted us to go to the Barnado's Home in Redcar, but the authorities would not let us. My sister and I were sent to an orphanage in Sydenham, London, and my brother to the Gordon's Boys Home – we didn't see him again for another twenty years. The Sydenham home was a row of houses and my sister was put at one end and myself at the other and we were not allowed to see each other. It was a very Dickensian regime, harsh and strict, our names were taken away and we were given numbers. We were beaten for things like moving out of the 'approved' position in bed.

During the war the children from the home were evacuated to Horley in Surrey. From Horley those of us that were over fourteen were sent off to our nearest relatives, whether they wanted us or not. We were given five shillings and a bundle of clothes, whether they fitted us or not, and packed off on a train. I was sent to my aunt in Shepton Mallet, who didn't really want me and kept me under similar rules to those of the orphanage. I didn't know that this would only last until I reached eighteen years of age, when I would have been turned out of the orphanage anyway, so I ran away when I was at that age. I tried to join the armed forces, but my eyesight was too bad so I went to a cookery college in Bristol. After three months there I was sent to Red Marley to cook for forty mentally deficient men who worked, on lease, on local farms. Apart from the warden I was the only female there. We had to lock every door behind us. I didn't want to work there, but as I was paid monthly I had to work my notice out. I ended up working in the YMCA in Longsmith Street, Gloucester which is where I met my husband to be, who had come over from Ireland to work for the War Agricultural Committee.

That's when my life really started. To start with we lived in Longsmith Street and then St Michael's Square, Gloucester, moving to Hardwicke on my twenty-first birthday in November 1945. It was a typical scattered village, but a pretty one, surrounded by fields in those days. Our first home here was a very small cottage in Green Lane and the lady next door held my baby whilst my husband gave me the big, old key to unlock the door. The cottage had one room upstairs and one down, with a tiny scullery, no cupboards and no plumbing. The water supply was from a well in our garden which we shared with four other cottages. That very large garden is now the site of the mobile home park. The cottage was also without any drainage or electric power, but gas was provided downstairs for two gas mantles for lighting. We used oil lamps upstairs and candles for secondary lighting downstairs. Our toilet, a 'family two-holer' was in the garden thirty yards from the cottage. A large chimney recess contained a small twin-oven iron range with an open fire and a long chain suspended over the top to which one secured cooking pots (cauldrons)

Bettina Brewis with baby Diane, who had just won first prize in the Baby Show at Quedgeley Village Hall.

over the open fire, quite medieval in fact. A stone floor and two small windows with iron bars completed what was, even in those days, very primitive accommodation.

Our neighbours were Mrs Leach, Mr and Mrs Curtis, then old Mr and Mrs Handley with Mr and Mrs Russell on the other end. When we first moved in we had only the baby's pram, cot and milk pan, we slept on the floor with a coat over us. When Mrs Leach discovered that she gave us an old mattress and we started a club account with Jack Walsley, who worked with my husband, in order to buy a blanket. We gradually built up the household from there. Things like coal and furniture were still on ration. We bought roofing felt to put on the stone floors and what was then Bon Marché sold second hand furniture on the top floor, so we bought a table and chairs. There was paint available then called 'lino paint.' It was only just developed and wasn't very good, it never dried properly. It was unsuitable for furniture but we painted the chairs with it anyway. We ended up getting stuck to the chairs and the chairs to the floor! It was hilarious really, we had a lot of fun learning how to build a home! I had always had to work by someone else's rules and had a lot to learn. Even after we moved to Springfield in 1950 I was still putting bits of newspaper in the outside toilet and keeping the toilet tissue for the one upstairs, that's how I had been brought up and knew no better.

Cherry Stack

Allotments

The residents here always had a fair amount of garden, and did their own gardening. In addition to that there were two areas of allotments here where you could take a plot. There was one down Pound Lane and the one on the Bristol Road.

Norman Sims
(b. 1921)

Happy days

My mum and dad did all their courting before they was married in Frocester, they both worked in Frocester Court, mother was in service there, and dad was a groom there. Eventually they married at Eynsham, which was mother's home. After they got married, they came back to Hardwicke to live at Ellis' Farm in Sticky Lane in 1909. They stopped there on the farm where dad was the farm bailiff. During the war he had to buy horses and all for the war people there. He left there in 1919 and moved to Elmgrove Road East, which was called the New Road in them days. They lived in the house, a new house it was, called 'Springfield', I think that's where Springfield Estate got its name from. I was born there in 1919. My bothers and sisters, there's three of them, were born at Ellis' Farm and the youngest brother was born at Springfield with me. I went to Hardwicke school, the same as my brothers and sisters did. We had to walk to school in them days. We used to laugh in the wintertime because the floods used to come, and old Mr Stowell, at Church Farm, used to get his horse and cart and put us all on and take us through the floods to school. School days were good, happy days.

Ivor Prosser

The day we moved to Parklands

In 1953, when the country was preparing for the coronation of Queen Elizabeth, my mother had more pressing things to think about. After more than twenty years of living in a small cottage in Longney, with no electricity, gas or running water, our family had been allocated a brand new council house at Quedgeley. The house was one of sixteen on an estate called Parklands, and we were going to live in No. 15.

Dad had arranged with one of the local farmers to borrow a lorry, and I watched with excitement as our things were loaded onto it. Then I was put in the front with mum and we were on our way. Compared to the cottage - to me, as a child of six and a half, the house seemed to be the size of a mansion, as I rushed from room to room, switching on lights, turning on taps and flushing toilets. I hadn't realised these kinds of things existed and everything seemed like magic. The thought that there would be no more trekking down to the end of the garden to use the loo - not the most pleasant of places, especially on a warm day in summer - was the thing that delighted me most but my mum was more pleased with the thought that there would be no more humping heavy buckets of water from the pump in the yard for all the family's needs.

After a few weeks most of the houses were inhabited and, to my delight, most of the families had children around my age. This was also an improvement on our home in Longney, because the houses there were scattered and once school was over I didn't usually see any children until the next school day. Here, though, there was always someone to play with, and I would push my doll's pram up and down the pavement in front of the houses with other 'mums' such as Susan, who lived at number two, Ann from number eleven and Patsy from number seven. My mum had also been making friends with the neighbours, Mrs Spencer, Parsons, Harding, Biggs and Dowdeswell, to name but a few. They were always called by their married name, as to have called them by their Christian name would have been considered presumptuous. The houses all had gas meters which took shilling pieces and mum soon became known as someone to be relied on for change for the meter, and she kept a jug in the cupboard for this purpose. None of the houses had telephones and eventually the post office

Emily Sims, just after the war, outside Apricot Cottage, Hardwicke.

erected a phone box outside our house which took four penny coins, so another jug for pennies was kept in the cupboard. We always seemed to have someone coming to the door either for shillings for the gas or pennies for the phone, and of course a natter while they were there.

We had been living in the house for about two months and there had been no sign of anyone moving in next door, but one day my mum told me that the following week an elderly lady by the name of Mrs Pritchard

Nelly Sims with Peggy Sims (Roche) and Florrie Sims (Dean).

that she had 'lost' the arm as the result of an operation. So began our time at Parklands, a council estate that managed to retain the village community spirit, and where my parents were happy to remain for the rest of their lives.

Margaret Tuckwell

Back to the country

I was born in Hardwicke but my wife, Elsie, was a Gloucester girl and she refused to come to Hardwicke. She was born over her grandmother's shop in the Bristol Road. We got married at St Stephen's church in Gloucester and when we first got married we lived in two rooms in Gloucester – but I didn't like it. I love the country. We were there less than a year. We came back to Hardwicke and bought a little bungalow. We needed £25 deposit, which doesn't sound much now, but then £25 was ten weeks' wages. It was a very nice house. We moved in in 1944 and lived there until 1970. Then we built our own bungalow – nights and weekends. We've been married sixty-three years now.

John Drinkwater
(b. 1915)

would be moving in, and this poor lady had lost an arm, but when I saw her I wasn't to stare or make any comment about it. This puzzled me, as I couldn't understand how anyone could be as careless as to lose an arm, and also why my mum had sounded so sympathetic about her. After all, if I lost anything, I was made to go and find it. I then became anxious at the possibility that my limbs could fall off without me noticing, and every night when I went to bed I would tug each arm and leg in turn to make sure they were secure.

When Mrs Pritchard moved in, mum took me round to introduce ourselves, and I tried very hard not to stare but, like all young children, my eyes were constantly drawn to the lady's sleeve which was pinned up on to the top of her dress. It wasn't long before Mrs Pritchard noticed but far from being upset or annoyed, she was quite happy to explain

An effective cure

Nowadays you go to the doctor's but you didn't go to the doctor's then – you treated yourself. My husband reckoned raw onions cured everything – whatever was wrong, it was a raw onion for him. He worked for the Post Office for forty-six years and he didn't have any time off sick – so it must have done something!

Marjorie Dobbs
(b. 1916)

A sad accident

At first the houses in Springfield were numbered differently. We were at No. 32, but then it was changed to 19 and that was permanent. There was building work going on all around us, cement mixers, bricks, cement, tiles, door frames, window frames and plenty of workmen to go with them all. As children we used to run in and out of the half-finished houses playing hide and seek, and some of the foundations were great for skipping on. I remember having a large china porcelain doll and she was kept in the sliding cupboards in the front room. One day, by accident, one of the workmen opened the door and she fell out onto the black floor tiles and smashed into little bits. He was very sorry and the next day he went into town and bought me a new one, but it was never quite the same.

Mary Sims

Out-of-the-way homes

I was born in 1915 on Acklow Hill, up from the ballast and across Longney Lane. There were three houses as I recall – the gamekeeper lived in one, we lived in another and I'm not sure about the other one. Then we moved down to the Old Hall. My father came out of the army and the only thing he knew anything about was horses and the only job he could get was on the farms, so we lived in some very out of the way places.

John Drinkwater
(b. 1915)

Master butcher

I was born in Hardwicke, but we moved to near Haresfield when I was a baby, because my father had to go to the First World War.

He'd been a master butcher in Hardwicke, but he had to give it all up and go to war in 1917. He supplied all the area with meat, and he had his own shop: his name was Thomas Murrell. But he had to sell up all of his business when he left. I was about five when he eventually came home – he had to stay away two extra years after the war finished – but I've got loads of letters and fancy embroidered cards that he wrote to me while he was gone.

So my mother, and the four of us children, (there were two more boys born after the war), moved to a little village called Colethrop, outside Haresfield. My grandmother, Mrs Jane Gardner, lived in Haresfield, where she kept the post office, and my mother moved to be near her. There were just about twelve small cottages in Colethrop, and four farms at that time – and there was a little chapel where my two brothers were christened. It was a wild life for the children – quite free and easy. There were

The Sims family at School Farm Cottage.

Not many people in Quedgeley and Hardwicke owned cars but Jack Wyer, the blacksmith, was a keen motorist and enjoyed taking his family on outings. The cars pictured here and opposite are from 1926 to the 1940s.

plenty of places to roam, and mostly horses on the road. You could go right down to the canal, to Parkend Bridge, and no-one would worry about you. You just came home when you were hungry. The canal was a focal point. There were tugs that pulled all the barges, which would carry timber and petrol. Mr Holder was the bridgeman at Castle Bridge. He'd open one half of the bridge, and then he had to go down to open the next bridge at the junction at Saul. One or two of the children who played down there did drown. One boy who I went to school with was drowned at the age of thirteen, learning to swim. I've never actually been on the canal – it's my ambition to go on one of the boats.

I can remember the local squire – Squire Tiddeswell. He was a very stern man, but very straight. The school used to go to him once a year, to have tea and games on the lawns – egg and spoon races. The boys would touch their caps to him whenever they saw him about – mind you, in those days they would touch their caps to anyone who seemed important. Squire Tiddeswell was killed in the hunting field, when

I was eight or nine – he fell off his horse. He was an older man then, in his seventies probably, and I remember all the older children in the school going to his funeral.

When I was ten, we moved to Moreton Valence, where my dad used to do his rounds in a horse and cart. Our home was called Yew Tree House, on the corner of the lane going down to the church. It was eventually pulled down, and there are new houses there now, but in those days it was thatched. We had an orchard, and my parents used to get cider made from the fruit. Once, we had it made at our house, with a big horse that walked round and round. Even we children used to have the cider when it was made first, because that was when it was nice and sweet. There were thatched sheds attached to Yew Tree House, and there had been a smithy in one of them, but he'd gone by the time we moved in – just the anvil was still there. My dad retired early, and the people who bought the house turned it into tea-rooms.

Nancy Davis
(b. 1915)

More of the cars owned by blacksmith Jack Wyer from 1926 to the 1940s.

Special permission

I used to live at Quedgeley when it was a proper little village, just fields and trees and a few little cottages dotted about. My husband Nick and I were married at St James church in Quedgeley. My dad, George James, used to paint the church clock back in the 1940s and '50s. He was a local builder, and that was one of his contributions to the church, to paint the clock in black paint and gold leaf.

My dad built a bungalow in Naas Lane, right at the top on the right hand side next to the railway line. You used to be able to go across the line there, but it's all been altered now. It was the last house, apart from the signalman's house. As kids we always used to go up there, sit on the gate and wait for the trains to go by. Of course it was all steam trains then. The bungalow is still there now – Lynton Fields. It was a lovely bungalow, and we had lovely gardens there. Being a builder, my dad had collected together all the materials to build the house, and then the war came, and he couldn't do it. And then immediately after the war there was a restriction on building, and you weren't able to build without special permission. So he wrote to Mr Bevan, he was in the ministry, and he explained that he had all the materials and it seemed ridiculous that he couldn't build his house. And he got a letter back, which more or less said: 'Carry on George!' So he built the bungalow.

Valerie Hodges
(b. 1933)

Bath time

In those days we had no central heating, bathroom or any of the luxuries people take for granted today. Washing was from a tin bath that mother would bathe me in alongside an open fire, which we'd also use to warm our clothes before we dressed.

I remember the cold mornings, the frost clinging to the windows. We drew patterns on the frosted surface as we readied ourselves for school before setting off with our bread and dripping sandwiches for lunch.

Richard Cale
(b. 1943)

A happy family

I couldn't face being in a house without children, I used to love it when they broke up for the school holidays. I cried all the way home when my first little girl started school. With my last two, both boys, I got the nickname of 'The Four Minute Miler', not that I could do a mile in four minutes! It was just that the second youngest could not understand why I was leaving him there and taking Johnny back home. He would kick and scream because he didn't like being left. Eventually the teacher, Mrs Robinson, said: 'Get him here just as the bell goes, I'll take him directly from you at the last minute and you run like ——'. So we got over it that way. It took him a long time to really understand why he couldn't come back home with us. He didn't like school meals either, and I was wasting money on those so I thought I'd make sandwiches. I used pastry cutters, hearts, clubs, diamonds and so on to make the sandwiches more attractive and he would eat them then.

I made an awful lot of mistakes in the early years, but I learned from them all and that made me a better parent. If I had had a normal upbringing, in a family, it would have been different. But being brought up in an orphanage where they took away your name and gave you a number, where the rules were so strict, I wasn't quite sure how to do a lot of things. None of my children were mistakes, they were all talked about beforehand. After the first I'd think, 'Poor little thing, she'll have no-one to play with.' And so it went on.

June Ryland (née Hooper) with young Diane Brewis, friend Jacqueline and two visiting Dutch boys.

There were two girls and my husband wanted a little boy. So then there were two girls and one boy, who'd have no-one to play with.

There was a five-year gap where I had no babies and the youngest was about to start school. I got myself into such a state worrying about having no baby to tend my doctor advised me to have another! Well, with the older ones all at school this new one would need a playmate as well. So, here we go again!

With what would have been my eighth child I had a kidney disease and the poisons killed the unborn baby. I can now understand about women who steal babies, perhaps after a miscarriage. I was friends with Nurse Powell's daughter, both of our babies were due at about the same time. With mine born dead I was in such a terrible state I would meet my friend and take the pram off her and run away with it. I was barred from the baby clinic, if I had found a baby left unattended I would have run off with it, that was the state I was in. That lasted several months, I really had to work at it to pull myself through. Children were my life. I was brought up in an orphanage with 200 children. When I was sent to my auntie she had children.

There were four children where I first worked in service and at the job after that. When we lived in St Michael's Square, Gloucester, there were children in the house there as well. So I was never really without children round me. I never believed in giving my children pocket money when they where growing up, they had to earn it. Two daughters and the eldest son used to deliver the *Citizen* all round Hardwicke and Quedgeley. Bob, who was at boarding school because of his health, used to come home at weekends and, with his younger brother, would collect all the papers up again. They would parcel them up and a company would come round and buy them off him. I can't remember the name of the people who ran the company, one brother was an athlete, quite a good one, and Mrs Davis' daughter, Dinah, was courting the other. After their father died some of them had jobs at Colethrop Farm, Mr Godsell was very good to them.

Yes, it was a hard life in the early days, but a very good one. We were a happy community, everyone willing to help each other. It was safe to go out without locking your door and the children could play safely in the road. Now I have my family, neighbours and friends caring and looking out me, there's nothing else I really want or need. I am very lucky.

Cherry Stack

A cold home

School Farm was the draughtiest, coldest place in the universe. I've had glasses of water by my bedside which not only froze, but which split the glass. And don't forget we had linoleum then, not carpet, so when you got out of bed you couldn't let your feet touch the ground for very long. And there was an outside toilet – up the garden, about half a mile away from where I was in bed!

Eric Vick
(b. 1929)

A rare tree

We left the bungalow in Naas Lane eventually and went to live with my Gran on the Bristol Road, which was only a small unlit roadway then, at a place called Beryl's Close. Every winter the show people would come and stay there. They had big caravans and they lived there all through the winter. They were very nice people. There was a lovely orchard there with a very rare pear tree; it was a very tall, Victorian tree and it produced pears every year, which were as hard as bullets but were absolutely delicious. And we used to have beautiful Victoria Plum trees, and mum used to sell the plums at the roadside.

Valerie Hodges
(b. 1929)

Friday fish

We would kill a pig and there was always plenty of pork and bacon. I can remember the bacon hanging on the kitchen wall and it would be that hard you couldn't stick a knife in it. You had to get a hacksaw to cut it. It was all salted in those days – no wonder we've all got high blood pressure! But there was no junk food in those days.

Every Friday we had fish. My mother would catch the bus at the top of the drive. I used to hate Fridays because she always brought back haddock, which was my father's favourite, and which I absolutely hated! And then of course there was everything out of the garden – when the first lettuce came through it tasted wonderful. You could only get vegetables in season – you couldn't get lettuce and tomatoes all the year round like now.

Eric Vick
(b. 1929)

Proper tea

Tom Fredericks was a major tomato grower, as well as flower plants for everyone. And he cut hair. His mother used to have me over for tea sometimes – proper tea, with real bread and home-made butter and nice jam.

Eric Vick
(b. 1929)

Moving on

I like living here by the canal – we have a big garden with lots of animals. We have three dogs and four cats, a rabbit , some fish and four birds. We had some ducks too – three girls and a boy. They had a little blue duck house in the garden, but they decided to live on the canal instead. They flew away and made a nest up by the bridgekeeper's hut near The Pilot. I like watching the boats too. I especially like waving to the passengers on the *Oliver Cromwell*.

Perdita Ashenford (b. 1995)

Diane Brewis in the garden of The Retreat, Quedgeley in 1947.

3 Shops and Trades

St Crispin, on the Bristol Road, where Charlie Smith's father and grandfather ran their bootmaking business.

The cordwainer's house

Grandfather made boots by hand sewing them, he was properly called a 'cordwainer'. When he was first married he came to live at The Star before it became a public house. Where my house, St Crispin, stands now (on the Bristol Road, opposite the turning to Green Lane) there was an old thatched cottage, a wayside cider house, where an old couple by the name of Meadows lived and sold cider to carters and the drovers who were driving their cattle along the road. Eventually the couple died and my grandfather bought the house and the piece of land for £50 and had the house taken down to build the present one in its place. All but one of his children were born in this house and the old man died here. My father learned the trade of cordwaining – bootmaking – and carried on the business. He was also clerk and Sexton at Hardwicke church and continued these duties right up until he had to finish work. I learned some of the trade but didn't really take to it much because I didn't like being shut in. I didn't like sitting down so much, working, so that was it. The old shop used to be on the end of the house. That was my grandfather's and father's workshop. They used to make boots for the salmon fishers at Longney and boots for farm workers in those days – heavy nailed boots, water-tight to the top, thirty shillings in those days, guaranteed good leather right through. It was my job to cut out the uppers and sew them up, and father put the bottoms on.

Our house got its name from a friend of ours that used to be in the Post Office and moved down to Newport. He was a long-headed sort of chap and he studied history for quite a long time. He found out that St Crispin, and St Crispinus, were Romans and the patron saints of sandal makers in their days. He thought that, being a bootmaker's shop, it would be nice to call it by that name, so he got a nice piece of teak wood and carved 'St Crispin' on it. It's now up on the front of my house.

Charlie Smith

A family tradition

I have lived on the Bristol Road, Quedgeley, all my life. Grandfather Fred, my father John Cale, my sister, son Jonathon and myself are part of a long line of Cales who have lived in Quedgeley through the years. My great-great-grandfather was married at Quedgeley church in 1819. His son, my great-grandfather, was born at Hempsted in 1828. My grandfather Fred, his son, was born in 1852. My father was a basketmaker in Quedgeley for sixty years, grandfather for seventy, alongside being a thatcher. He was still working on roofs until his late eighties – he died at the age of eighty-seven. He was also the village gravedigger for twenty-one years! His son, my father's brother Charles, was killed during the First World War at Ypres. His name can be found on the war memorial in Quedgeley churchyard. He was one of many in the Gloster Regiment that fell on that day 4 October 1917.

I myself was born and raised as a young boy in Quedgeley in the late 1940s-50s in the bungalow which was home on the Bristol

St Crispin, the 'cordwainer's house'.

Above and opposite: The many thatched cottages in the area kept thatcher Fred Cale very busy.

Road. Father bought the bungalow for £20 in 1926 and brought it across the fields at 3am on a trailer from Manor Farm to its resting place on the Bristol Road. And that's where it stood for the next sixty-two years.

Richard Cale
(b. 1943)

Delivering bread

There used to be a baker who came round, Hawkes at Quedgeley. There was a man with a horse and cart, and a man with a van. In the evenings after school I would go in the van and help him, delivering the bread in the village and at Harescombe and into Haresfield. After the round, if we went back to the bakery, he would get me a cake or a loaf of bread to take home - it was lovely bread. Sometimes I would walk back home along the Bristol Road. I suppose I was about eight or nine.

Eric Perkins
(b. 1934)

The Hawkes brothers

In Elmgrove Road East, in the last house on the left coming down from the Morning Star, lived Mr Hawkes, a baker. His bakery was on the old A38 (Bristol Road) in a large wooden building, with a tin roof, situated almost opposite Tesco. There were two Hawkes brothers and they always delivered their bread on a horse and cart as well as selling it from their own house. You could smell the whiff of lovely baked bread as they drove places on their horse and cart. My mother often sent me up to their house to buy a loaf, and I remember getting a clip across the legs as I had to explain why I had bitten a big chunk out of the end of the loaf.

Mary Sims

Beautiful bread

Hawkes the baker used to deliver bread late at night – he was always known as the Midnight Baker. You left your basket on the doorstep and he would put the bread in it – it was beautiful, crusty bread. You could smell it as you got close to the bakery. And the fruit and veg man used to come round. If he didn't have something mother wanted on the Saturday, he would bring it round on Sunday morning.

Valerie Hodges
(b. 1943)

The midnight baker

During the war there were no buses. I had to walk from Quedgeley into town to do my shopping. My mother used to live on the Bristol Road, so I used to walk to my mother's, then we would go around the town and do our shopping, then I used to come back to mother's and then walk home. It would take about an hour to walk into town. It was a straight road. We had no shops, only Hawkes the bakers. That was just along where Tesco is now, only the other side of the road. They mainly did bread and cakes, nothing else. They had a baker with a horse and trap and they used to come round. On a Saturday, we used to call him the Midnight Baker because he was an old man and he used to go to sleep in the cart and the horse would take him home. The horse knew the way better than him. You couldn't see the man – just the horse taking him home. We used to say, 'Here comes the Midnight Baker!'

Marjorie Dobbs
(b. 1916)

Gloster Aircraft Company

My wife Valerie and I both worked at Moreton Valence which is where we first met. It's a very historic place, Moreton Valence airfield, which

Road farm, Bristol Road, Quedgeley

The Mk 1 Vulcan bomber taking off from Moreton Valence airfield runway – now the motorway. Robinswood Hill can be seen in the background.

The Mk 1 Vulcan Bomber at the Gloster Aircraft Company site, near where Blooms Garden Centre is now located.

not many people are aware of. The first jets were flown from there. I think the Gloster Aircraft Company purchased it or leased it mid-war time. Up until then it had been used by the RAF as a training area, so it always was an airfield, right back from the 1930s. When I worked there, there were a lot of Nissen huts and you could read on them where the pilots had to 'collect your parachute, check your equipment, check your oxygen and sign your two elevens' to say they had done this before taking off in their planes. I started working there in the 1950s. I started working for GAC at the main Brockworth factory and served my apprenticeship there as an aircraft engineer. There were about 20,000 people working there then. I then moved down to Moreton Valence. It's all gone now – they built the motorway down the runway. The Javelin was there, and I worked on the Meteor. There were more than 400 people working there at the time. There was a service department, a research department, the experimental department. The Queen actually landed there back in the 1950s when she visited Gloucester. Everything was smartened up for the visit.

They built a brand new hangar there, called the Kelvin hangar. It was beautiful, with a polished floor, cafeteria, everything. Then as soon as it was finished, we were all made redundant. That was in 1962, and the place shut down.

Nick Hodges
(b. 1933)

The village postman

My dad, Vic Charles, moved to Gloucestershire in 1932 and came to live, with his family, in a small cottage in Lognney. They had moved from their home in Wales so that my father could take up the position of postman covering the villages of Hardwicke, Quedgeley, Longney and Elmore. Each of these villages had its own small post office and general store, but the one at Quedgeley was also the dropping off point for the mail from Gloucester for all four villages and was run by a Mr Parsons and, in later years, by his daughter Lilian. Dad would cycle every morning, from Longney, to be at Quedgeley in time for the delivery of the mail from Gloucester. Then he and his colleague would sort the mail in the shed in Mr Parson's garden. Once this had been done it was time for the two men to start their rounds, one doing the deliveries for Quedgeley and Hardwicke, and the other doing deliveries for Longney and Elmore. On alternate weeks they would swap rounds and so Dad became well known in all four villages.

Before the Second World War the villages were very different to how they are today. There were no large housing estates and your 'next door neighbour' could possibly live a mile away so often the postman was the only visitor some of the villagers saw all day. However, most of the villagers knew everyone, not only in their own village, but also in the other three, and as there was little means of getting very far afield, very few ever ventured beyond the boundaries of the four villages, so many of them were related through marriage. The postman was therefore looked upon as a vital link between the communities and dad's 'duties' far exceeded those laid down in his official terms of employment. It was quite usual for him to be invited in to someone's house for a cup of tea while they finished writing a letter that they wanted him to deliver for them. If this was on his route it was taken for granted that it would be postage free. But if it was going further afield, dad was expected to have enough stamps in his wallet for them to buy and so save them having to make an unnecessary journey to the post office, and he always made sure that, before starting on his round, he had sufficient stamps in his

Vic Charles, the village postman, with his daughter Margaret on her ninth birthday in 1955, outside 15 Parklands.

wallet to cover these eventualities. Letters and parcels weren't the only things though that dad was expected to deliver. Quite often he would be seen, on his bike, with a pair of rabbits hanging from the handlebars, or a basket of fruit balanced precariously on top of the carrier at the front of his bike. These were the things that parents wanted taking to their sons or daughters who maybe lived a mile or so away or in the next village. Dad was never one to refuse a cup of tea - he regarded the villagers as his friends and it would have been impolite to refuse. The fact that these frequent stops made him late back at the delivery office didn't concern him – everyone knew how prone Post Office bikes were to punctures and faulty valve tubes!

In 1939 Dad went to war serving as a Petty Officer in the Royal Navy, but as soon as he was demobbed he was back doing the work he loved best, delivering mail. It wasn't long after his return that the area acquired a post van, which the two postmen shared on an alternate week rota. dad was now able to extend his personal service to his customers by delivering eggs, milk and even flagons of cider from one village to the next, and one of his favourite delivery places was at Joker Bennett's at Elmore Back. Joker was well known locally for his home-made cider, and on several occasions dad was called upon to act as taster to Joker's latest brew. It was on these occasions that, later in the day, my mum had to do her best to salvage letters that had been covered in spilt milk caused by dad's erratic driving through the country lanes after sampling Joker's cider. It says a lot for the regard that the villagers had for my Dad that no-one ever complained about him to the Post Office but, after all, there were very few that he had not helped out in some way over the years, and the feeling of friendship was mutual.

In 1958 dad suffered two massive heart attacks and had to give up work for twelve months. He was then only allowed to return if the Post Office would agree to him having continual use of the van. To begin with this was allowed, but they ruled that it had to return to the alternate week system. The doctor's refused to allow dad to ride a bike and so he was forced to retire.

A few months later the Head Postmaster for Gloucestershire presented Dad with the Imperial Service Medal. The inscription on it reads 'For Faithful Service' but whether that was to the Post Office or the villagers of Longney, Elmore, Hardwicke and Quedgeley is a matter of opinion!

Margaret Tuckwell

Making hay and cider

Hay making and corn harvest was a busy and interesting time when I was a lad. The grass was cut with a mowing machine drawn by two horses. After cutting it had to be turned and shaken out to dry, then raked up into rows called wallies. After this it was put up into haycocks which stood in the field until dry and then the wagons came and took large loads to be stacked in a barn or made into a rick. The corn harvest was a very interesting job. When it was ripe a machine was brought into the field. This machine cut the corn and tied it into bundles called sheaves and threw them out into the field. The sheaves were then stuck up into stooks to finish drying. When dry the corn was taken to the farm on wagons, some being stored in barns and some built into ricks. These were built on raised platforms called staddles – a ring of stone pillars with timber placed on top. This was done to prevent rats and mice getting into the rick. Cider making at the farms has been carried on in the Severn Valley for many years and was the recognised drink on all the farms and in many cottages. There were orchards on all farms and the apple trees bore fruit for cider. Mr Stowell at Church Farm used to make hundreds of gallons every year. The cider was made in a cider mill. This was a large circular trough with a large stone wheel running around in it. The wheel was driven round by a horse which walked round and round. Apples were placed in the trough and the wheel crushed them. When they were crushed enough the pulp was taken out and spread on a hair sheet on the press. Another sheet was laid on top and more pulp and so on until the required height was reached, then a large board was placed on top before the screws were screwed down. The juice from the fruit ran out into a trough and was carried away and put into large casks and allowed to stand until it was ready to be corked down.

Charlie Smith

Special delivery

Flooding was not infrequent in the proximity of Hardwicke church and the old Parochial School. I frequently paddled, bare foot with my skirt tucked up, with the water over the axles of my large wheeled pram, as I delivered newspapers door to door in that area. If the water was too deep I would leave the papers in a certain place and someone on a tractor would collect them.

Cherry Stack

Farming land

We had a village shop run by a Mr and Mrs Davis, their daughter Doris and her husband Bob Andrews. It was a little white building in the grounds of their own land. Doris and Bob lived across the road in Springfield. Their daughter, Dinah, had horses and used

The floods of 1947 made travelling difficult.

to tend them out in the adjoining fields. Mr Davis had quite a few fields alongside his shop where he used to keep milking cows and pigs. There was a big black shed back in the fields, where the doctor's surgery and shop are now in Westbourne Drive. We often played in that old shed, but if the cows were out we used to think twice. All the fields where Elmgrove Estate and St Nicholas Court are now were divided by wire fences. The wire fence was replaced by a big wooden fence opposite Springfield and we used to spend hours walking along the top of it. We fell off more times than we stayed on! Open fields ran right across to Green Lane Pond – a ploughed field (Ploughman's Way), a corn field (Cornfield Drive) and a field of grass, clover and buttercups (Clover Drive) – all names for the fields were suggested by Charlie Smith who lived on the Bristol Road opposite Green Lane.

Mary Sims

An absolute fortune

After school I went to work for Listers in Gloucester for a twelvemonth in agricultural engineering and then George Downton, who was the landlord of The Pilot, offered me one and sixpence an hour to drive a tractor for him, doing agricultural work. The first week I was corn cutting and I earned £10, which was an absolute fortune because I was only ever getting £1 less stoppages for my work at Listers. I did that for a couple of years and then my uncle was taken ill and I went down to run his farm, which was a council-owned farm, at Standish. When he died they wouldn't let me have the farm. I was very glad afterwards that they didn't although I created at the time. My uncle had a car and trailer which he used for hauling cows for his neighbouring farmers, and my aunt gave me the car and trailer, which is how I started in haulage. In between market days I used to help Jesse Vines out with his threshing, with his threshing tackle, going round the farms.

The blacksmith's shop at Four Mile Elm in Hardwicke in 1922.

Jack Wyer's blacksmith's shop.

There were lots of land girls in those days on the farms – so it was a good way to get an introduction!

Eric Vick
(b. 1929)

Many trades

In the period between 1925 and 1940 we had a coal wharf where boats came down the canal and off-loaded there, and Jack Taylor delivered coal to the people in Hardwicke and district. We had a builder, a chap named Bill Butler, who did building work around here, and had his workshop on Hardwicke Green in the barn that at the moment is being restored into living quarters. We had a cobbler or shoe repairer, Jim Smith; we had a blacksmith – that was my wife Evelyn's father; we had a carpenter/wheelwright, opposite the blacksmith's shop, which was run by Mr Peyton, who was also an undertaker. We also had a bus operator, and he also had a charabanc, as it was known in those days, that was Bill Gardner. We had a slaughterman who, when residents had a couple of pigs and it was time for killing, would come along and kill the pig. We had a baker, in Quedgeley, that was Hawkes Brothers. As for milkmen, we had milkmen delivering milk, there was Harry Smith who lived in what we called the 'new road' in those days, but of course is now Elmgrove Road East; Perce Davis used to deliver milk and subsequently John Charlton used to deliver milk. He came to the door with his churn of milk and he had a pint can and you took your jug out and that was poured in. We had a weekly delivery, if you required it, of fruit and vegetables. Priday used to come round the village. If you wanted groceries, then Vicks, who were provision merchants at Frampton, would deliver them weekly.

The blacksmith's shop at Four Mile Elm

Looking back we had so many different trades. Subsequently we had Harry Say with coaches, he was in the same place that Mal Witts now is. We always had a post office here in the village, run by a gentleman named by Mr Davis. He was always known locally as Dapper Davis and that was in a house just past the junction of Church Lane, and then subsequently that came up to Drivers, which is another house along here where there was a shop and post office.

We also had a shop run by Mrs Stephens up on the Bristol Road. And when we were at school, Mrs Herbert in Stank Lane had all these bottles of sweets. We used to pop over from school and she used to come out from doing her washing, her hands all wrinkled, and put these sweets in paper cones. The pubs were the same – Morning Star, Cross Keys and The Pilot. We had a doctor's surgery here, but that was a surgery in a private house. The doctor came from Stonehouse, three times a week, Monday, Wednesday and Friday. Locally, we always had a midwife, Nurse Tracey, in School Lane, Quedgeley.

Norman Sims

First time on the 'phone

In those days there were no telephones – news getting from one to another was just word of mouth. I remember when I became a foreman and I had to use the telephone and I'd never used one before – I was terrified! Not like today when the kids are brought up with them. The telephone exchange was on the end of Pound Lane and Evelyn Sims was the operator.

John Drinkwater
(b. 1915)

Getting a hair cut

Tom Fredericks was at Hardwicke Bridge – he was there a long time, for forty-six years, and he knew everyone, he knew whole families. He used to cut people's hair, men and boys, and we used to get sent down there to have our hair cut. It was the old thr'penny bit that we had to pay. Most locals used to have their hair cut there, in a little cabin, by the gate.

Eric Perkins
(b. 1934)

Working hard

The pace of life was slow and gentle, but the work was hard and unrelenting, most villagers were connected in some way with work on either the surrounding farms or the RAF storage depots. Hardwicke was a separate community from Quedgeley, the only economic link being Hawkes bakery, near what is now the Tesco roundabout, which supplied both villages.

To start with my husband was only earning £2 10s a week, but the farmer, Mr Manners, paid the rent for the cottage, he was a marvellous man but could only do so much for us. So I had to find work for myself. My first job in Hardwicke was at Hardwicke Farm where, adjoining the milking sheds, there was a small dairy where I worked. I used to take my baby with me and, while my late husband John was milking the cows, Vera Heyward and myself used to wash and sterilise the milk bottles in two big galvanised tanks. Then, after the milk had been poured over a cooler, a thing like a big metal wash-board with cold water flowing inside, we would fill the bottles using a jug and then put the cardboard disc on to seal the bottle. We had to work fast to get it done ready for the milkman, Fred Dennis, to deliver it. If my baby wanted feeding I had

Blacksmith Jack Wyer with one of his creations.

to go into a little shed to feed her. A group of us ladies used to plant potatoes by hand, in the furrows made by the tractor at Colthrop Farm, in Haresfield, for Mr Godsell. As they grew we would have to hoe between the rows until, later in the year, our children came with us to pick up the potatoes, loading them into sacks. It was hard work but we enjoyed it.

At other times a coach would come to take us and our children out Newent way, to go fruit picking. There were blackcurrants, gooseberries and strawberries to pick. Anything to earn a few pennies.

I had to keep working to make ends meet. My husband's wages had gone up to £3 10s a week by the time we moved into Springfield, but the rent of £1 a week made a big hole in that. The children's allowance helped, but not enough. I always found a job where I could take the babies along with me, except when I cleaned the offices for Trentham's, the builders, who had offices on the corner of Naas Lane, where the BT depot is now. When I worked there in the evenings I could leave the children safe with my husband. Mr Trentham was a good employer and didn't mind my bringing the children with me when I worked there at weekends. When he learned that one of my sons was interested in engineering he sponsored him to go to college and gave him a job afterwards. After my husband contracted cancer he worked there for a time as well. I also cleaned for Mrs Winters, the wife of the headmaster of Quedgeley school, that's the old primary school that used to be at the top of School Lane, where the Community Centre is now.

Cherry Stack

Starting work

I was one of nine. I went to Linden Road school and I left school at thirteen. I had a job in a shop. Not many people went on to

sixteen – you had to be very, very clever to go on to sixteen. Holidays and weekends we were allowed to stay out all day. Mum would give us some sandwiches and a bottle of pop and we would go out for the day.

Marjorie Dobbs
(b. 1916)

Local tradesmen

There were five tradesmen in Hardwicke carrying on their own businesses. They were my father, who was a boot maker, Mr Lyes, who was also a boot maker, Mr Austen Brooks, butcher, Mr W. Coole, blacksmith and Mr M. Peyton who was a carpenter and wheelwright and also the local undertaker. All these men earned a living in the village and the surrounding district.

Charlie Smith

Employment

From a working point of view in this village in those days the men were mainly employed on farm labouring. In those days although it mainly all belonged – and still does – to Hardwicke Court there were about ten individual farms that were operating so there were quite a number of fellas employed on the farms. They were all tenant farmers. And there was a little bit of employment on the Gloucester Sharpness Canal. Timber used to be brought up from Sharpness, up to Gloucester where there were many timber yards. There was employment there. Some of the people worked at the Gloucester gasworks, as it was known in those days. My father worked there.

At Hardwicke Court there were gardeners, grooms, estate workers and servants, so there were quite a number employed there. And of course, subsequently, there was 7MU started

The Old Hall, Hardwicke.

and took a lot of people. That didn't start until 1938/39. It was the RAF Maintenance Unit, and they kept all the supplies there for the officers' mess all over the country.

Norman Sims
(b. 1921)

A versatile man

Tom Fredericks was a wonderful gardener. He was very versatile. He used to make fruiting ladders, and he used to cut people's hair. It used to cost four pence. It wasn't much of a haircut, but it saved going to Gloucester! When he retired and left, everybody missed him because he was so useful to everyone. If you wanted a dozen cabbage plants, you always went to Tom Fredericks. If you wanted a bunch of flowers for anyone, you always went to Tom Fredericks.

John Drinkwater
(b. 1915)

Purple plumes

The landlord of The Pilot was Mr Phelps and he had four black horses, and he used to do funerals. These four black horses would all have a purple plume – I remember seeing them when I was a lad. Ordinary people didn't use them though, we used to push the coffin down to the church on the bier.

John Drinkwater
(b. 1915)

The estate carpenter

Nora Franklin's father was the estate carpenter – he used to make all the gates and all the stiles and the hunting gates, and every one has WF on – Walter Franklin – he burnt it on with a brand. There were about three or four fellows then on estate maintenance, and all the gates were made at Hardwicke Court, underneath the Court. Miss

43

Bert Sims, pictured just after the war.

Olive showed me under there once. There's a big cellar, and inside there were lengths of wood – I'm not sure now if it was oak or elm – and she said 'that's for the repair of Hardwicke Court'. They were all laid out on the trestles. Miss Olive was also an authority on septic tanks – all her cottages were on septic tanks – and she could talk on septic tanks! She was an amazing lady – she would have made a very good MP.

John Drinkwater
(b. 1915)

Lovely bacon

Opposite the Old Hall is the Red House, that was a village shop. They used to sell lovely bacon. My Dad used to kill a pig every year; we used to sell half and keep half ourselves.

John Drinkwater (b. 1915)

The village dairy

The farm along the lane (Sellars Road), on the corner, just this side of The Pilot, that was the village dairy. Miss Selina Sparrow – her name is up in Hardwicke church – she and her sister ran the dairy. They made cream, cheese, butter and all. They had the old-fashioned patters with different motifs on; it was lovely butter. Eventually they passed on, and it was turned into the village slaughterhouse.

John Drinkwater
(b. 1915)

General stores

When I was going to school there was, pretty well opposite the Old Hall, a shop, like a general stores, kept by Mr and Mrs Margaret. It was in the Red House, in what I suppose is the kitchen now. People went there for groceries, cheese, sugar, butter and things. They sold ha' peths and pennyworths of sweets, all packed up in paper bags, and we used to get these long pieces of black liquorice with a hole through the middle. Mr Margaret sold paraffin and things like that, and he used to drive round with groceries at night in an old pony and trap. There was a path at the back through the fields to the church, but the lane was exactly the same as it is now.

Charlie Smith

A special flower

My husband was paid to cut the grass in Springfield, which he did with a scythe, and all the local children loved that time for they played with the grass and made dens in the piles until the council took it away. He also looked after the churchyard. There was a place in the churchyard where a little blue flower grew that Olive Lloyd-Baker used to like, so he had to be careful not to remove that.

Cherry Stack

Local shops

A family named Davis had a smallholding opposite Dutch House, now Hardwicke Newsmarket and Post Office, and they used to have hen houses along this side of what is now Hildyard Close. We had hen houses there as well until the new houses were built. The Davis's also had a little general shop that they opened when the shop on Bristol Road closed. Mr and Mrs Vallender had a shop in Dutch House and ran the Post office there and, when that went up for sale, the Davis's bought it and their daughter, Doris Andrews, ran that shop, enlarging it a bit. Mrs Davis and Mrs Andrews couldn't do enough for

people, when my husband was in hospital having an operation for cancer they were marvellous towards me. The Davis's old shop then became a barber's and finally a DIY shop before closing down for good. The Dutch House then passed on to the Smiths, who enlarged it a bit more, and then to the Sparrows who enlarged it even more and had the car park put in. The Sparrows were lovely people as well. They took over in 1986 and, during a storm in the same year, the Dutch House was struck by lightening and the whole top of the house was burned out. This was after my husband died and my brother was living here. My then partner and myself were on holiday at the time and my brother rang us up at Bournemouth and said if I didn't mind he'd asked the Sparrows to stay with us until the house was repaired. That took about six months. We gave them the dining room as a sitting room and one of the rooms upstairs. All my children had left home by then.

Cherry Stack

An outing sets off from The Morning Star.

A job in engineering

I went to school until I was fifteen, nearly sixteen, and then I got a job in an engineering shop. I stayed with engineering the rest of my working life, until I retired at sixty-two. I did thirty-nine years with the Ministry of Defence, some of that time spent at Quedgeley.

John Drinkwater
(b. 1915)

Wedding flowers

Keith and Andrew Cowan of Green Farm in Sticky Lane provided the village with cucumbers, tomatoes and chrysanthemums. They provided all the flowers for my wedding bouquet in 1969. Bread was delivered by Stan Hawkes from Quedgeley, and meat was delivered on a Wednesday by Len Tomlins.

Anne Hocking (née Willis)
(1947)

Stunt driver

Dick Sheppard, the stunt driver, was at Gloster Aircraft Company – we were apprentices together. He had a great big American station wagon and he used to take us, every lunch hour, down to the Morning Star. He used to charge us sixpence – we used to get a tremendous cooked meal for sixpence. Dick used to get his meal free because he had taken us all down there. He became quite famous eventually. Later, when my son Richard was at Beaufort School, he came round the school and gave a talk. He brought his stunt car and did stunts in the playground. His famous racing car was called Mickey Mouse, and it had a big picture of Mickey Mouse on it.

Nick Hodges
(1933)

4 Around the Villages

Great-grandfather's diary

My great-grandfather kept a diary – I've still got it in my possession and it is very, very interesting because he worked on the farms in Quedgeley and he recorded when they started mowing, when they started and finished haymaking - some time in July or something of that - and when they went on doing different things. In the middle of all this he would put down the date that someone was buried - he used to record that in his book you see because he was there as clerk. And when somebody's child was christened - that was down in the book along with various other items like, towards the winter - about November – 'killed the pig' ready for winter. People were very, very self-reliant and self-supporting to a great degree, they grew their own corn and potatoes, killed their own pig and things like that.

Charlie Smith

Testimonial to Miss Harris

After her twelve years' residence in Hardwicke, and successful tenure of the post of headmistress of the National School, it was only natural that some little token of the affection and regard in which she has been held by all her classes should be given by the parish to Miss Harris, on her leaving to take another and a more important school.

Through the willing and zealous energy of Miss Preen, representatives from almost every house in the parish placed their names upon the list of subscribers. On June 16 at 8 p.m. a meeting was held in the schoolroom, and was attended by Mrs Barwick Baker, the vicar and Mrs Nash, Mr and Mrs Cozens, and many of the parents and children. The vicar said he had been entrusted with the task of making the presentation to Miss Harris, and that he did so with feelings of very great regret, for he was well aware of the excellent work that had been done by Miss Harris, and the love in which she was held by the several generations of school children who had passed through her hands. He hoped, however, that the change would be for her benefit, and that she would meet with kind friends, a happy home, health and strength, and much professional prosperity and success, under God's blessing, in the performance of the new duties she was about to undertake. He then asked her acceptance of the testimonial which consisted of a purse containing £6 0s 6d, together with the list of names of those who had subscribed towards it. Miss Harris made a short reply, expressing her sorrow at leaving, and her gratitude for the kindness shown to her. The school will re-open, under the new mistress, Miss M.E. Hawes, on Monday 27 July.

From the Standish and Hardwicke Parochial Magazine *July 1896*

Militia on Quedgeley Green

My grandfather was born in Quedgeley in one of the old cottages that are at the back of the church. His father worked on the farms round about there and was also clerk of the

Miss Olive Lloyd-Baker.

A soaking for the organist

Hardwicke church used to flood in those days and I remember one Sunday night, when all around Hardwicke church was flooded and you couldn't see where the road was and where the brook was. This young lady brought the organist, Mr Braithwaite, down to play the organ. He got out the car and raised his hat to her and stepped back – and next thing, his hat's floating off down the brook. He was soaked!

John Drinkwater
(b. 1915)

Potatoes for lunch

There was no resident clergyman at Quedgeley in my grandfather's day and they never knew when there was going to be a service on a Sunday. One of the bellringers used to go up into the tower and look out towards Gloucester. When he saw the clergyman start galloping across the green he would come down and start ringing the bell for the service to call the people to church. The old clergyman used to go into my great-grandfather's house to have his lunch, and if they were having potatoes for their dinner he would say: 'Mary, if I may have one of your potatoes?' to go with whatever he was eating. When he had had his lunch he got back onto his horse and trotted down to Hardwicke church for the afternoon service, on to Moreton Valence to take Evensong down there and then rode back to Gloucester.

Charlie Smith

Remembering neighbours

In 1940 we lived at Quedgeley, at The Retreat. There was the playing field, then a row of houses. One was lived in by Mr Mansfield,

church. In those days Quedgeley church was on the village green, which then reached from Upper Green Farm, where Mr James the horse dealer lived, right down to where the BP depot is now. This was all common land belonging to Quedgeley and in those days the old Gloucester Militia used to come down and drill on the green. The Militia were dressed in three cornered hats, frock coats breeches and stockings, had a bow tied in their hair hanging down the back of their neck and carried muzzle loading guns. Now all of these men had to have good teeth because their powder was wrapped up in grease-proof paper - they had to bite the paper, pour the powder down the muzzle of the gun and then ram it, with the paper on top, down the barrel with their ramrod.

Charlie Smith

the shoe repairer. Next door but one was the post office, in the house, which was kept by Mrs Parsons and her daughter Marjorie. Then there was Mr and Mrs Smith and their family. In the end two were two sisters, Mrs Oliver and her sister, who were very elderly but still used to do all their own gardening. Then there was scrub up to where the village hall is now. Opposite the village hall was a little shop and behind it was the bakers, owned by the Hawkes family. I used to take my daughter in her pram to get the bread – and if I didn't watch it she would eat it on the way back! The baker used to do a round on a Saturday, lardies and Chelseas and that sort of thing, and if he didn't finish the round on the Saturday he would come back on the Sunday with a little hand cart.

Bettina Brewis
(b. 1922)

A head for heights

When my grandfather was going to school there were steeple jacks working on Quedgeley church. Whilst they were away having their dinner one day he went up the ladder and moved the cockerel on top for a bit of fun. He always claimed that he was the only one, barring the steeple jacks, that ever went to the top of the church.

Charlie Smith

A funeral fright

Quedgeley churchyard contains a large vault where the Curtis Hayward family are buried. They were the Squires of Quedgeley, owning the majority of farms and land in the village. When one of the family passed away it was Grandfather's job to open the vault, clean it and prepare it for the burial. On one occasion the funeral of a Squire was taking place and the bearers brought the coffin down into the

Hardwicke Court.

Hardwicke Court, pictured during a recent village fete.

vault. However, there was a problem as the coffin would not lie correctly on the shelf and to rectify this one bearer came back to correct it. As he did so he felt a hand on his shoulder and a voice asked if he required a hand. The voice belonged to Gramp! The bearer went white with fright and fled up the vault steps in terror! Father told me later this was the last funeral this bearer attended! The story went that Grandfather was in the vault and was taken by surprise by the arrival of the mourners. In order to stay inconspicuous he remained hidden in the large vault and unintentionally took the unsuspecting bearer by complete surprise. It's hard to imagine the churchyard like that these days. Back then it was a bleak place surrounded by fields, elm trees, and with a small shed where the chestnut tree is today. The shed may have been there

from the Victorian days of Burke and Hare to guard against body snatching – something that all village churchyards had a problem with at that time.

Richard Cale
(b. 1943)

Village nicknames

Everyone had a nickname, no-one was called by their proper name. There was Shunty Smith or Steam-Easy Collier. He always called me Jerry which I used to hate as a kid because that's when the war was on. Everyone in the village had a nickname.

There was Shackleton Philips – that was because when the chimney was on fire, he climbed up there and shoved a great big clod of earth on top of the chimney. It put the fire out but his mother had a great big pot of stew down the bottom, and the dirt fell down into the stew. So he got the name Shackleton from the shackle pot, which always had everything shoved in there by the end of the week.

Eric Vick
(b. 1929)

Potato fields

Every year Mr Stowells used to plant two fields off Pound Lane with potatoes. Anyone in the village could buy a row – about 200 yards long – for £1. You could dig them when they were young potatoes or leave them in until the end of the growing season. You had to be there on the Saturday morning and he would plough them out for you. Then you would pick them up and put them in sacks and he would take them home for you on his horse and cart. They were lovely spuds.

John Drinkwater
(b. 1915)

The first bus service

Quedgeley's very first bus service was a horse bus. It was so slow you could jump on as it passed by. Along the Bristol Road near the old gasworks there used to be an old stone trough for the horses to drink from and on its side an inscription read 'Drink and let no man hinder you'. The trough is now outside the Waterways Museum in the docks. Father said not many people would use the horse bus because of the high fare – 3d return, in old money. The horses themselves were changed at the Talbot Hotel in Southgate Street, near where the old Severn Sound studio building stands. The passenger stop was outside the old Walwins Chemist, now also closed. Quedgeley's motorized bus service started in 1912 and was initiated by William Gardner, landlord of the Morning Star pub in Hardwicke. The price of a ride was one shilling and the route stretched between Frampton Green and Gloucester. Mr Gardner's daughter worked as conductress and the buses in those days were 'utility.' Besides having wooden seats there were also no windows and the only

The Old Thatch, Church Lane.

protection from the elements were side blinds which could be drawn down from the ceiling. The bus could seat thirty but on busy days it wasn't unknown for passengers, parcels and luggage to occupy the roof space too! Solid tyres and poor roads made the going rough too. There were two buses running the route until finally Mr Gardner sold out to Bristol Tramways. My grandfather frequently used the buses when he was thatching houses on the Clifford's Estate, Frampton.

Richard Cale
(b. 1943)

A special phone call

Miss Lloyd-Baker used to ride around the village in her pony and trap, wearing a big green cape. Not many people had phones in those days, but we had a Post Office phone. One day she knocked on the door: 'Use your phone?' she said and walked in. I was nursing my little boy. 'Yes,' I said. She used the phone. 'Thank you', she said, and off she went. My husband said: 'Did you ask her to pay?' and I said: 'No, of course I didn't. She practically owns the village!'

Marjorie Dobbs
(b. 1916)

Gardens at Hardwicke Court

When I was fourteen I went to work at Hardwicke Court, in the kitchen gardens. I learned my gardening under Mr Tarling, he was there for quite a time. He retired when I came back out the army, after my National Service. Then we had another head gardener, called Mr Taylor and he was there for quite a time before he moved on somewhere else. Then we had another one – I think his name was Mr Jeckylls – and then he left and then Fred Swain came with his wife Joyce

and his children, Sheila and Martin. He was head gardener and I was under gardener. The gardening involved everything – fruit, vegetables, a walled kitchen garden and a big garden outside - and we did grass cutting. We all mucked in and did everything. There were greenhouses with peaches in and figs and grapes, and tomatoes. We used to grow a lot of dahlias and chrysanthemums and bush roses, and there were two big herbaceous beds. We used to grow a lot of flowers for the big house, because Miss Lloyd-Baker liked fresh flowers every day. We used to show at a lot at local shows. Hardwicke Show was in August – it was a big thing, and planned well in advance. Hardwicke Court always had prizes, for potatoes and fruit and flowers.

Every year we used to dress the church with greenery, sometimes at Easter but always at Christmas. We always decorated the lychgate as well. Eventually Fred went to Staffordshire and I ended up doing everything – gardening, washing cars, and the forestry. Then in my last two to three years there I totally switched to forestry until I got made redundant in 1968.

Eric Perkins
(b. 1934)

Growing our own

Our back garden was all planted with vegetables, the lady next door could not cope with her garden, so we had vegetables in that as well. Added to these was a garden across the fields, belonging to a Mrs Cale with even more vegetables and a row of potatoes in a field at the farm. We needed all that to feed ourselves and seven children! Between looking after the children, cleaning and doing the housework I used to make my own bread, and when there was a strike I would make it for the neighbours as well, from flour they supplied, and some to sell in the local shop. Two of my sons worked at Dow Mac, on

Naas Lane, and their workmates asked them where they got their bread. I ended up making a few more loaves for them to take to work. We would get through twenty-eight loaves a week in the family, but sometimes I made up to fifty-six a week!

Cherry Stack

Life At Hardwicke Court

When I was a lad we used to go down to Hardwicke Court, my mother was very friendly with those down there because she used to be in service there. They used to sell dripping - good beef dripping, sixpence a pound. You'd see the cook cut it out of a big bowl and there was all the jelly underneath. Sixpence a pound, I've fetched many a pound or two when I was a lad. In those days Hardwicke Court was always full of company. There was the family - the old Squire, Mr Michael and Colonel Arthur Lloyd-Baker and there were the girls, the ladies. Two or three of them hunted and the stable yard was full of horses - all the horseboxes were full. There were four or five staff in the stables, and seven or eight in the gardens. Old George Rodmans was head gardener when I was a lad. They had a cricket team, it was very good; Hardwicke Cricket Team always played at the Court. We used to go down there and mow with a horse mower and roll the pitch with a big roller drawn by a horse.

Charlie Smith

A close encounter

My cousin, Brian Townsend, was on his bicycle coming down Naas Lane one day with a friend when a UFO, in the shape of a ball of fire, virtually chased them down the lane. They were terrified. The backs of their shirts were all burned. It caused quite a stir, and it was reported widely

Diane Brewis blackberry picking on the canal bank.

at the time, both in the local and in the national press. They never came to any conclusions as to what caused it. This was in the late 1950s. They had quite a lot of correspondence with certain people over it, and it was registered as a UFO of some kind – but they never discovered what it was.

Valerie Hodges
(b. 1943)

Real country

In the summer, in School Lane, the trees would meet in the middle over the lane and you could walk all the way down to The Pilot. It was lovely, real 'country.'

Betty Brewis
(b. 1922)

Hardwicke church choir in the early 1940s.

Church duties

My father, James Smith, was verger at Hardwicke church for many years, and also grave digger. The church in those days was lit by oil lamps which had to be filled with oil every week. The church was heated by a boiler burning coke. When I was old enough I had to help Father in these duties. In the winter I used to go to stoke the boiler on Saturday nights ready for Sunday. In those days the church was always well attended. People did not mind walking, although some did come on bicycles.

There was a good choir of men, ladies and boys who sat in the chancel where the organ was then. Mr Risbey was the organist and cycled from Gloucester twice, on Sunday and Wednesday nights, for choir practice.

Charlie Smith

Church links

The church was the main focus of the village. The school which we all attended until the age of eleven was tied to the church. We attended church as a school on major feast days, such as Ash Wednesday.

Anne Hocking (née Willis)
(b. 1947)

A surprise pancake

The organ at Hardwicke church was up in the chancel and Mr Risbey, the choirmaster, used to ride his cycle from Gloucester on a Wednesday night to hold choir practice, and twice on Sundays. He used to come to my house on a Sunday morning, practically every Sunday, because he had a shop in Stroud Road, the post office, and they used to sell various things. They used to sell eggs and my mother kept a number of fowls and he used to have the eggs off us. He always carried those eggs in a net bag and he seldom broke one, unless he got a soft shelled one. He'd put them in the bag and pick it up, if he heard one crack he'd have them all out on the table and find the cracked one. He used to laugh about one Sunday when he got just about by the gasworks and he was cycling along very nicely with the big string bag full of eggs, about two and a half dozen, when some vehicle came and swept his hat off. He always had to use the step to get onto his bike and he tried to put his foot back on the step but his foot slipped off. Down he went in the road with the bicycle and his eggs. He had a right mess and, he said, he picked them up in his hands. He could see some of them were alright, but the yolks from the broken ones were running through his fingers. He went into the Gloucester garage and said to the fellow there: 'Get your wife to make a pancake with them'.

Charlie Smith

Foot and mouth disease

I remember when we had foot and mouth disease in the village. I watched them burn the cattle at Hardwicke Farm. I don't know what year it was, but I was very young.

John Drinkwater
(b. 1915)

Making hay

We moved to Hardwicke when they built the council houses. There was a field which ran down to Dimore Brook, with cowslips and primroses. There was no main road or street lights. Mr Lyes' place was half way down on the left, Cornfield Drive is where he kept his pigs. You walked from Elmgrove Road East to Elmgrove Road West through three fields. You could then walk down Elmgrove Road West to The Pilot. From Elmgrove Road East to Green Lane there were fields – perhaps belonging to Hardwicke Court Estate.

The Forge on the Bristol Road in Hardwicke.

Percy Davis kept one of the white cottages, opposite what is now the post office, and ran a smallholding. He used the fields for his cows and pigs. When it was haymaking, everyone would help. The children loved it, helping to turn the hay. It would go on for a week or more. At the end of the evening his daughter would come out with large trays of bread and cheese and spring onions, with squash for the children and cider for the grown-ups and the children would have a last ride on the horse and cart.

Mr Davis also kept chickens and if the fox got in and bit the heads off the chickens, he would dress the bird and give it to you. Sometimes you would find a bag of firewood on your doorstep. We used to go over with a jug and get milk – you can't do that now! Mr Davis' daughter, Doris, started a little shop at the side of the house. Eventually she moved over to the big house and took over the post office. She would cut bacon on the machine, and so on. In 1973 she moved out. Apart from the post office and the bakers you had to go into town to do your shopping. Everyone would help everyone.

Bettina Brewis
(b. 1922)

Salmon fishing

Father and I used to go over to Longney in the season to see them salmon fishing at Mr Browning's, and do you know, you could get a salmon then, what they called a botcher – that was a partly grown salmon, only a young one - but if they had a good botcher, about seven or eight pounds, they'd sell him. Father knew Mr Browning, the owner of the fishing draft, very well because we used to work for him, make boots for him and his fishermen. Father would say: 'Have you got a small fish Mr Browning?' and he'd reply: 'Yes we've got one up at the farm', and he'd go up to the

farm with us. He'd come down every evening and take the fish off the fishermen, take them back and put it in the cellar, on rushes, to keep them cool you see. He'd say: 'Ah! There's one up there, about seven or eight pounds, and you can have it for 1/6d a pound'. We'd had several from there, we used to have a Severn salmon - a whole fish - my word was it good.

Charlie Smith

Dusty roads

When I was at school, our house, on the Bristol Road, was on a level with the road which in those days was scraped by the old roadman with an ordinary scraper. They used to put the stone down on the road and pour water on it from a water cart. Then the steam roller came along and kept going backwards and forwards, grinding the stone down until it was solid and hard and leave it wet. Then of course, it would dry out and the few motor cars on the road in those days threw up a column of dust, the houses were filthy. The dust got in the windows and doors and everything was covered in a white dust. The hedges and all were white with dust in those days, until the Tarmac came along. Then, of course, they stopped scraping the road and the road gradually built up until now I have to come down two steps from the road into my house.

Charlie Smith

A new home

I was in the land army; my husband worked for Post Office Telephones. Where the nursing home is, St Vincent's, just before the roundabout in Hardwicke, I lived opposite there – there were some cottages. My husband was doing the telephones for Mrs Witchell that lived in the cottages – when the RAF came she used to do sandwiches and dinners for people in the shed at the side of the garden. She was going over the road to the big house and doing it there so the cottage was empty. So my husband asked her if we could have the cottage, so we got married then and went to live there. Now the cottage is knocked down and the thatched cottage next door is knocked down. They've got three big houses there now. We had no water, we had to get the water out of a hole in the field; we had no sewers. It was normal then – they didn't have the sewers along Quedgeley then. It was a bit of a job washing day and bath nights! Still we had a garden and I had chickens and things like that.

Marjorie Dobbs
(b. 1916)

Getting around

There was a bus at the Morning Star in those days. Old William Gardner was at the Star and he had an old Alford bus. It was open all the way down the side, it had a top and a ladder up the back and it had solid tyres. I know the first day Bill had this bus delivered, I forget now whether it was George Nash or young Bob Gifford had the job to drive. They went for a joyride one Sunday morning, down as far as Sharpness and back, some of the privileged customers from the Star were invited to go. They went down to Sharpness and had a drink and then came back. He used to run from Frampton-on-Severn to Gloucester and Bill Gardner's daughter, Ivy, was conductress. They'd fetch anything you wanted from Gloucester and there were boards around the top of the bus. The top of the bus was flat and they put all the stuff up there. Ivy had to climb up the ladder onto the top of the bus to get your parcels. Then he got a better bus after, one with pumped up tyres on. But, before then, there were carriers' carts from

Frampton. There was old Mr and Mrs Fryer, they used to run from Frampton and charge 3d to go to Gloucester. You could stand by the side of the road and watch them coming, stand for about five minutes before they got to you because the old horse was going jogging along. Old Mr Fryer, on the front, was nearly asleep and the old lady was sleeping peacefully in the back. She was acting as conductress and you had to shout to him and he'd pull up, go round the back to wake the old lady to get in when she opened the door - a poor old lady with a veil over her face.

There were also two boats on the canal, the *Wave* and the *Lapwing*. They used to run from Sharpness to Gloucester, up and back every day, and they'd stop at any of the bridges and pick up people. People used to send their goods down on them and they were dropped off at the bridge where they wanted. It was very, very nice. Those two old boats were commandeered for the First World War, I don't know what they did with them. Afterwards the government had to hand them back, and they came back all right and I remember a big naval tug brought them up the canal. There was this great Naval vessel about four or five times as big as the *Wave*, and he was towing the old *Wave* along behind like a little cockleshell. He had to deliver her back to Gloucester.

Charlie Smith

Life at the post office

By the time of the war, my mother was on her own running the shop and post office at Llanwern in Sellars Road. Her friend Valerie Morse from the village became her assistant. My mother and father had three daughters, Christine - known as Mary - born in July 1943, Helen born in 1946 and me, Anne, born in 1947. The shop and post office was the hub of the village and therefore we met up with most people, but there was never any gossip. My mother was involved in most things in the village, including the Mothers' Union and the Women's Institute, and she was very friendly with the vicar, Dr Stacey Lewis and also Miss Olive Lloyd-Baker. They were both frequent visitors to the house. Miss Olive Lloyd-Baker was the Lady of the Manor. She was benevolent, gentle and someone who earned the respect of those in the village. As children we visited Hardwicke Court quite frequently, and she drove a Bristol car that she called Buttons. I also remember Mrs Dolly Smith, who lived at Sellars Farm with her husband Ted and their two daughters Pamela and Margaret. Dolly and her friend Mrs Cale were the two ladies who 'laid out' the local dead of the village. They travelled on their trusty bicycles and when you saw them together you knew what was afoot. Then there was Ted Smith, who was a wonderful ditch digger and drove a wonderful old blue lorry.

Albie Sims, of Apricot Cottage in Church Road was the grave digger. He was a great character and used to yarn about the Reformatory and all the boys. Mr Root, the policeman, lived in The Police House on the Bristol Road, opposite Green Lane. He caught me riding two on a bike and I recall I lost my Rowntrees Fruit Gums into the canal. His wife was a hairdresser - pudding basins were the order of the day! I also remember the gypsies and their painted caravans camped on Hardwicke Green – as a child I found them fascinating.

In 1954 my mother was taken seriously ill with a brain haemorrhage. She was admitted to Frenchay where she underwent major surgery. My sister Mary kept the family home ticking over while we younger girls went to stay at Panholme with my aunt. The post office remained for some eighteen months or two years with Margaret Smith in control. Unfortunately the Post Office insisted that my mother relinquish the post office and it was closed and moved to Springfield where it remains today. The Vallenders ran the it initially. My mother returned home to Hardwicke paralysed, and not the vibrant lady that she had once been, but the village rallied round and supported the family.

Anne Hocking (née Willis)
(b. 1947)

Percy the pig

The farmer used to get lots of orders for cockerels for Christmas, which used to be one of the main Christmas meals in those days. My husband would bring about a dozen home and we would pluck and prepare them and take them back to the farm. We had a little piggy to look after, the runt of the litter, that was funny. The farmer asked my husband to bring it home and nurture it. Well, I had never had anything to do with animals, the way I was brought up, so, since I fed my babies held in the crook of my arm I'd put the piglet in a blanket and feed it the same way. In the end he wouldn't have his bottle unless I was holding him. We called him Percy. The others in the family could move about and he wouldn't react, but if I merely moved a foot he was alert. When the rent-man came I had to shut him in here and meet the rent-man at the gate, that pig was more like a dog! When he got to a certain age he had to go back to the farm and I really missed him. After that though there were several other animals to look after. Where the TV is now there was a cupboard and my husband put a board across it and straw in the bottom and we kept chicks in there until they were old enough to go outside. We had linoleum on the floor then and, in the evening, we would let them out to stretch their little legs – and then had fun gathering them all up to put them back again!

Cherry Stack

A village tragedy

One family that featured prominently in my childhood was the Wall family. Mrs Wall had taught at Hardwicke school as a supply teacher. Mr Wall worked at Fyffes but had been torpedoed in the war. They had two children, John, born in June 1947 and Helen, born in 1951. We spent Christmas, usually Boxing Day, either at their home, the thatched cottage opposite the side gate of the church, or at our home. We also used to go to Christmas pantomimes, in a large group. John passed his 11-plus and went to The Crypt, Helen passed her 11-plus and went to Ribston. But in 1967 the village was shaken by a tragedy, which affected me tremendously. John had apparently shot his mother and father and then waited for his sister to return from school, and shot her. He then turned the gun on himself and the dog. The dog was the only survivor.

When the family was found, John was still alive, but died shortly afterwards. Their funeral remains with me. Seeing four coffins brought into Hardwicke church was devastating. They are buried on the left hand side of the main footpath going out to the lychgate.

Anne Hocking (née Willis)
(b. 1947)

5 Hardwicke Reformatory

Reformatory School

The Reformatory was there when I was a child. This school, at the other side of the canal, was built a long time ago, being first thought of by Miss Olive Lloyd-Baker's great-grandfather. It was a very strong built brick building to accommodate young boys who had committed various crimes. I remember the boys used to come to church twice on a Sunday, morning and evening. They marched up from the Reformatory through the back door of the church in those days and sat in two blocks of seats. In winter the monitors walked alongside with gale lanterns, old paraffin lanterns, and their drill instructor, Aaron Rogers, a former sergeant out of the army, was in charge of them. They were always trying to drown out the village choir. Of course they were a lot of big, strong, boys and they'd sing as loud as ever they could on purpose. They were formed up by Church House when they came out of church and had to call-off by numbers, 1,2,3,4,5 right the way down. They knew how many lads they'd got and if one ran away there was a number missing. The run-away would vanish into the churchyard, hide behind a tombstone or something, and clear off. If you caught a runaway in the village you had two shillings, and if he was outside the village you got two shillings and sixpence. Sometimes these boys, once now and then, were never found, they'd been known to swim across the Severn, get into the Forest of Dean, and vanish – go down the pits or something like that.

Mr Walkley was land-master at the school and he used to tell the tale of taking two boys out into the fields to put them to work to dig a ditch out and trim the banks up. They started work and he went to do some other job and supervise something else. Later on he came back and found no boys, only two spades. Eventually the Reformatory closed and Mr Walkley took Madam's End Farm and went farming on his own. He used to tell the tale of milking one afternoon, just as usual, when all of a sudden a voice said: 'Good afternoon Mr Walkley' and he looked round – there was a soldier stood there, a man of the Artillery. Smart looking chap, he was, with a cane under his arm, spurs on and all that, and he was clean and tidy. Mr Walkley said: 'Good afternoon, I don't know you'.

'No. I don't suppose you do sir, but I know you, oh yes', replied the soldier. 'Do you remember taking two boys out into a field and putting them to dig a ditch at the old Reformatory School?' 'I do', Mr Walkley answered. 'What did you find when you came back?' asked the soldier. 'I found two spades but I never saw those boys again'. 'No', said the soldier. 'I was one of those boys'. He had run away you see, and he made good. Those boys, a good many of them, the better behaved ones, used to be lent out to the farmers to do hoeing and haymaking and things like that. They went out to Colethrop Farm, to Mr Chamberlain's, he always had two or three, and they'd go back at night. They were charged for the use of them. The boys dressed in corduroy trousers and jackets during the week and on Sunday they had navy blue suits with brass buttons down the coat.

The Reformatory, Hardwicke, near School Farm.

There's a memorial plaque at the back of the church organ in memory of those who were killed in the First World War. I forget now how many boys were killed.

Charlie Smith

In Memory Of The Reformatory Boys
The memorial tablet in St Nicholas church, Hardwicke reads:

This Memorial was erected in memory of Those old boys of Hardwicke Reformatory Who fell in the Great War 1914-1918 whose names are inscribed hereon and in thankfulness for the safe return of the 243 other Old Boys of the School.

Astbury, A.
Butcher, W.
Cull, A.
Gilligan, C.
Hayes, H.
Houghton, A.
Jones, C.
Loveridge, W.
Midgley, J.
Norris, C.
Partridge, G.
Rowe, J.
Schofield, N.
Simmonds, H.
Taylor, W.
Thomas, J.
Williams, G.

Reformatory's war record

When the war came in 1914, Hardwicke Reformatory answered the call most gallantly. Twelve of the older lads at once enlisted, and at the close of hostilities the proud record of the Institution was as follows:

Members of Committee serving – 5
Members of staff serving – 3
Ex-Inmates in HM Navy – 12
Ex-Inmates in HM Army – 245
Ex-Inmates in RAF – 3
Killed in action, 3 members of committee, 10 ex-inmates; died of wounds, 5 ex-inmates; died from sickness, 1; wounded, 79; gassed, 3; missing, 2; prisoners of war, 8.
Distinctions gained: 2 MM and 3 DCM

Of voluntary and gratuitous war work done by the boys may be mentioned: 861 oat-sacks made; 4,750 grenade bags made; 16,032 individual hours' work put in at National Filling Factory on Saturday afternoons.

Extract from the Reformatory's records

Bombs and billets

The boys from the Reformatory had to work on the farm under the strict supervision of a Mr Robinson, a very hard task master, and a couple of equally strict masters who lived in the cottage across the field. Behind the main building, heated by coal and log stoves, was another building used as the laundry. Everything was washed by hand, put through old wooden mangles and then placed on long metal tails on rollers to dry. Upstairs was the ironing room. There was a large dome on the main building with a large bell to bring the lads to order. The coal was brought along the canal by long boats, tied up at the wharf and the boys had to carry the coal up the front drive (about 600yds). This was only one of the hard tasks set for the boys. At the outbreak of the First World War very many of these lads went to fight for their country, in Germany and France. Sadly not many returned to finish their sentences.

Around 1922 the Reform school was closed down. Later on, in the 1930s, Miss Lloyd-Baker turned the place into a riding school. In 1939 the Second World War started and all available buildings were taken over to house evacuees from the large towns to get away from the bombing. A party of mothers and children came to stay from Birmingham, but alas they couldn't stand the quiet. They preferred to go back and face the bombs. Later, about 1940, a section of RAF lads were billeted there. They looked after the searchlights and barrage balloons in the area until the war was over. Later still the scout movement met there twice a week. The top floor was used for a ballroom and village dances were held there. But as the building was so far out of the village, and across the other side of the canal it became more appropriate to use the village school. Later on, in the 1950s, Priestley Studios used the premises as their warehouse for a while.

Mrs Florrie Dean (née Sims)

Spam everywhere!

As a small boy I remember the Reformatory when it was full of RAF. They were there through the main part of the war, running a decoy across the fields. The idea was that it was lit up like a factory and the intention was to draw the bombs there. It didn't work – unless it worked that day when they dropped the seven bombs. Then they filled the Reformatory with Spam – the whole place. There was hundreds of tons of Spam in there – upstairs, downstairs, everywhere. We got fed up with Spam.

Eric Vick
(b. 1929)

D-Day alert

During the war, all the fields in front of Hardwicke Court, and Quedgeley Court were full of vehicles. Hundreds of them. That's how we knew when D-Day was, when they all started to move out at once. At least, we guessed it was going to be something big, we didn't know it was D-Day then.

Eric Vick
(b. 1929)

An injured knee

I remember the Reformatory when Miss Olive Lloyd-Baker had it changed into a menage. I remember it because in the course of doing that work there was a heap of broken concrete. My uncle was a labourer on Mr Vick's farm there and we youngsters – Florrie Sims and Les and Peggy – were running about there and I ran over this heap of stones and hit my knee. I went up to my auntie and she bandaged it up and put some ointment on it. Subsequently I developed blood poisoning and I went into Gloucester Royal Infirmary, as it was then, in Southgate Street, and I was in there for twenty-eight days. I've still got the marks now where they operated on my knee.

Norman Sims
(b. 1921)

Boy Scouts

The Church Youth Club was in the Reformatory – we used to enjoy dances there. To dance we had to sprinkle crystals on the floor to make it slippery. And of course the Boy Scouts used to be there. The Boy Scouts were run by Peggy Jones, who was Miss Olive Lloyd-Baker's companion; she was assisted by Austin Goodman, who she subsequently married. We used to go up on the top floor.

Norman Sims (b. 1921)

Demolition

When we first moved to the Bridge House I was five years old and my sister Portia was three. We used to live near a busy road, but here we had a huge garden, loads of fields and, of course, the canal. But our favourite building was the old Reformatory. We used to make up stories about the boys who were sent there, and try to imagine what it was like to be sent away from your family to this big, strict school in the middle of nowhere. The building was old and empty and quite spooky, so we would make up ghost stories too. Once we thought we had even seen a ghost. One day we came home and noticed that just about all the windows in the Reformatory had been smashed out. There was glass everywhere. We weren't allowed to play near it after that, and soon afterwards it was all boarded up so no-one could get in and look around it any more.

Then a man came and took all the tiles off the roof. My mum asked him if the building was going to be knocked down but the man said no. He said it was going to be done up and converted into flats or something. But nothing else happened and the Reformatory stayed without a roof so all the rain and weather could get in. I remembered my mum telling me about when she was a girl living in Stroud and some people wanted to knock down the old buildings in the High Street. Other people wanted to keep them so they sat on the roofs and in the end they persuaded everyone that the buildings should be saved. Lots of people were interested in the Reformatory but no-one sat on the roof to save it.

It was knocked down in the spring of 2001. We watched the men take it down, brick by brick. It took quite a few days. They took the bricks away to use them again somewhere else. Now there is just a big empty space where the Reformatory used to be, and it still seems strange, when we come home, and the Reformatory is gone.

Morgan Ashenford (b. 1988)

6 On the Canal

Boat building

I remember they made concrete boats in the First World War, opposite the gasworks on the side of the canal. Nichols & Co. built them and they were made of a steel framework with shuttering outside and in and then wet concrete was poured in. They built ships of solid concrete, but they were never a very great success. One or two of them foundered and sank and went to pieces. There was no engine in them, they used to tow them. I remember the first one - we went up to see the first one launched, she was built on the bank, alongside the road by the gasworks, and had to be launched broadside into the canal. They couldn't go bow first or else she'd jam across the canal. So they had to slide them down broadside. They stopped people going down the towpath because they knew what was going to happen - there'd be a big displacement of water when this great thing went into the canal - so they put a barrier across above and below. People were all out in the Bristol Road waiting to see, but boys, they will be boys, and they dodged past the policeman and went down the other side of the hedge out in the fields - right opposite where this boat was going to be launched. There was a big blackthorn hedge there - a great tall hedge - and there were these boys laid down and you could see this row of faces through the bottom of the hedge. All of a sudden the word was given for the launching to take place. They shoved the lever over and in she went - whoosh - just like that. A big displacement of water went up in the air when

she went in, very nearly emptied the canal just there. The water went up in the air and came down smash, right on top of the hedge where the boys were. They were very near drowned! The hedge collapsed with the weight of the water and these kids went up the path. So that was the launching of the first concrete ship, that was about 1915, early in the First World War.

Charlie Smith

Barefoot

My eldest, a girl, was born five weeks before we came to Hardwicke. In those days I went barefoot everywhere, and encouraged my children to do so as well, except when they went to school. In the summer, on our way to Hardwicke Farm, we would go over the bridge by the Pilot Inn and paddle in a natural stream that ran alongside the road. I used to take my children to watch the barges on the canal, there were many then, loaded with wood and coal etc. We would also go to the crossing on Naas Lane to watch the steam trains go by. We would go for picnics as well.

Cherry Stack

Life as a bridgeman

When I left school I took several little jobs in Gloucester until I found the right one. I went to work for John Newth, the electrical people, in St Aldate Street. I worked there for a bit, and then I went to work for Moffat's the timber merchants. In them days you had a job to keep jobs, they kept making you redundant. And then I went and worked for the Gloucester Welding Company. And eventually I finished up as a bus conductor for the Bristol Tramways. My father was appointed Bridgeman in 1935, and as the house came with the job we all moved to the Bridge House at Hardwicke with him. It was called the Gloucester and Sharpness Dock Company, a private concern in those days. He retired in 1945 and I was given the opportunity to take over from him, which I gladly accepted, and my wife and I moved into the Bridge House. In those days we had no electricity, lighting was by oil lamps and the heating by coal fires. The coal was brought by longboats, five tons at a time, and was paid for by stopping two shillings a week out of our wages, which were fifty-four shillings a week then. The hours were 7.30 a.m. to 7.30 p.m., seven days a week and we had four days off a year, we had no bank holidays off, not even Christmas Day. If a boat did come on Christmas Day, which they often did, they gave us an extra shilling! A man used to ride down the canal from Gloucester, with a Gladstone bag, to pay all the men. When he packed it in he told the boss, 'Ivor'll take the money down for you if you want, his wife can look after the bridge.' So I had to ride down from Gloucester to Sharpness on my bike and they paid me ten bob for doing that, but we were glad of it. Sometimes boats came in the middle of the night, and we were paid an extra shilling a craft after hours, but only up to ten craft, then it reduced to sixpence. If it was dark we had to light four oil-lamps, two red ones to go either side of the bridge when it was open and a red and a green one to go either side of the canal. Life on the canal was very busy then, with at least six steam tugs operating up and down the Sharpness to Gloucester. The barges were

Diane Brewis sitting on the bridge at Elmore Lane.

loaded with various cargoes such as timber for Griggs and Price Walkers, timber merchants in Gloucester, Bass logs for Morlands Match Factory and also grain, spelter, tea, bricks and monkey nuts for the warehouse in the docks. During the early years that my father worked the bridge the long boats were pulled by horses, and I used to help him. When the horse came to the bridge the horses didn't stop. The man on the boat would unhitch the rope from the front and I would pass it over the bridge and drop it back to him on the other side. The farmers would bring their milk, in big 17 gallon churns, down to a landing stage and the boats would take that and sugar down to Cadbury's factory at Frampton-on-Severn where they made chocolate crumb to take back to Bourneville. We used to give

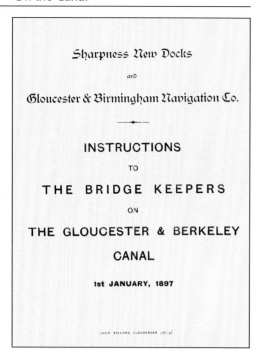

Instructions issued to Bridge Keepers on the canal.

Bungalows by the water

A little further along from the Hardwicke Bridge House was a cottage belonging to Hardwicke Court, and along from there was a caravan, and a small bungalow where some people lived for thirty years. They planted lots of trees and shrubs, which are still there. Beyond that there was another bungalow, and opposite that on the other side of the canal was another bungalow. They've disappeared since the bridge has gone.

Eric Perkins
(b. 1934)

The cabin in the pines

I learned to swim in the canal. Mum and Dad had one of the wooden holiday cottages. We called it The Cabin in the Pines. We used to go down there and have a swim – we

the men on the long-boats a half dozen eggs and they'd give us a little packet of chocolate crumb, a little perk of the job. We all kept fowls in those days and the men on the grain boats would give us the sweepings for our birds in exchange for eggs. We earned little money and the only way of making a shilling or two for Christmas was to keep a few cockerels to sell off. We used to keep a few pigs, breeding sows, to sell off at the market. There was an orchard at the back as well. The longboats also traded in coal and other cargoes. In the 1940s, '50s and '60s oil became a very popular trade with companies such as Severn & Canal, then came John Harker's and Shell-Mex. The cargoes ranged from 250 to 1,000 tons. These large boats were loaded at Swansea and their destinations were Quedgeley, Gloucester or Stourport. The number of boats coming up and down was about twenty to thirty a day.

Ivor Prosser
(b. 1919)

A letter offering Ivor Prosser the position of bridgekeeper at Sellars Bridge.

all learned to swim in the canal. The barges used to go up and down which was a nice sight – a whole row of barges going up and down. They used to bring the timber and the cattle feed up to the docks. There were a couple of boats that did trips – *The Wave* and *The Lapwing* – you could have day trip to Sharpness. There were some tea rooms at Sharpness and some swings, and that was an outing for us – it was gorgeous.

Marjorie Dobbs
(b. 1916)

Holiday homes

Away from the bridge, along the towpaths towards Gloucester and up in the fields, a number of chalets and bungalows were built. Some of these were used for holiday homes and, during the war and for a while after,

these were let for people to make a permanent home. As they had no water or electricity they used to come to me for water and paraffin for cooking, lighting and heating. I used to sell the paraffin to them, the chap brought it to me in five gallon drums. Then he said: 'I've got a two hundred gallon tank at the depot, I'll put that in for you'. Well, that made it easier for me. In the late forties and early fifties prisoners from Gloucester Prison, with a warder, would come as work groups to do bank clearing, towpath repairs and general work along the canal. One of these parties went missing one day and the warder set out to search for them. They had not gone far, only up into a field where they were found enjoying the favours of two 'ladies'!

About fifty years ago, a chap that lived over the bridge and his nephews used to come fishing. One day one of the lads came up to

In the mid-1950s, Sellars Bridge was demolished in an accident.

Holiday homes along the canal.

me and said that he thought his uncle was dead, they had been fishing up past the wharf, about a mile up the bank. I wondered how we were going to get him back, an ambulance couldn't get up there. So I went back and got my wheel-barrow, sat the old boy in it and pushed him back down the bank!

Ivor Prosser (b. 1919)

A very nice garden

There was a whole string of buildings along the canal. They were mainly wooden huts used as holiday homes. People would come and stay in them for a week or so during the summer. Mainly they were local people, from Gloucester, business people. There were a couple from Birmingham. There was also a retired policeman who lived there with his wife and they kept a very nice garden.

Eric Vick (b. 1929)

A keen fisherman

Our family lived in the centre of Gloucester. My parents also owned what I suppose could best be called a cabin on the banks of the canal at Hardwicke. We weren't rich multiple property owners or anything of that sort – the canalside dwelling was what would be regarded as pretty basic these days. It was made of timber, a small flight of stairs led up to a terrace where we could sit out on deck chairs. Inside there was one room and a narrow kitchen. The room served as lounge, dining room and bedroom. There was a very primitive lavatory outside. Almost certainly my parents had bought the cabin because Dad was an avid fisherman. We would visit the cabin at weekends in the summer and Dad would spend all day fishing, returning to the cabin only when called for meals.

Mike Sheridan

Accident at the bridge

When I first moved to the bridge it was made of wood and operated in two halves, the bridgeman opening one side and the travelling passman opening the other. This passman rode on a bicycle along the towpath, going from bridge to bridge from Purton to Hempstead in all winds and weathers. When they were short of a man they'd ask me to do that job whilst the wife looked after the bridge. I got ten bob for that. When the very large coasters started to trade with Gloucester, with all sorts of different cargoes, they needed two Passmen who were known as 'Hobblers' to come with them. Of course they were very slow and their draught of up to 12 ft made them difficult to handle and manoeuvre through the bridges. It was the Hobblers' job to guide them with the aid of ropes, as well as trying to prevent them from running aground on the shallower side of the canal. Sometimes the inevitable happened and one side of the bridge would be damaged by one of these large boats, or even knocked off. When this happened the carpenters would cycle from Saul Junction, carrying all their tools in a bag over their shoulder, to repair it with the aid of a steam crane brought from Gloucester by tug. In 1957 one of the coasters collided with my bridge knocking one half completely off into the canal. It was then that the company decided to replace it with a single span steel bridge that could be operated, hand wound, by one man. During the year it took to replace the bridge I operated a ferry across the canal for those needing to cross to get to work and to the Pilot Inn. When I first took over the bridge was named 'Sillers Bridge', afterwards 'Sellars Bridge', but it commonly became known as the Pilot Bridge after the Pilot Inn.

Ivor Prosser
(b. 1919)

The award-winning garden at Sellars Bridge.

The garden which won a prize for the Prosser family

Shopping by boat

My mother used to go shopping in Gloucester on the *Wave* or the *Lapwing*, which went up to Gloucester Docks. There were no buses then – I didn't see a bus until I was ten. Then Mr Gardner, who was proprietor of the Morning Star, bought a bus which used to run between Gloucester and Frampton.

John Drinkwater
(b. 1915)

Listening for boats

I grew up at School Farm, where I was born. My brother John and I came across the canal every day to Hardwicke School and we used to listen for the boats blowing. Then John and I would come down ever so slowly because we knew once the bridge was open, it would be open for ages. They used to send the barges

down then with one towpath man in front and one behind so no-one in between could shut the bridge. So even if the barges had got spread out you still had to stay there. So we could be there for a good half hour easy, sometimes even longer – with a bit of luck. So we had all the excuses in the world for arriving late.

Eric Vick
(b. 1929)

First bathroom

The bridge houses were very nice, we had a sitting room in the middle and a bedroom at each end, with a kitchen built on as a lean-to, but we had no bathroom or indoor toilet. In '64 I think it was they knocked all the back down and built three new bedrooms and a bathroom on the back and turned the front into a kitchen at one end, dining room in the middle and a sitting room at the other end. Before that we had a little room, an outhouse, on the end of the wash house. So I said to my boss: 'I can turn that little room into a bathroom'. He said I could and the company laid drains in for me to a cess-pit. That was the very first bathroom in a bridge-house on the British Waterways. That bath, as far as I know, is still in use at the bridge now, they put it back in when they rebuilt the place.

Ivor Prosser
(b. 1919)

Legendary bridgemen

Three bridges were worked by legendary bridgemen – Elmore Lane Bridge by the Priday family for 125 years, Ivor Prosser at the Pilot/Sellars Bridge for fifty years, and Hardwicke Bridge by Tom Fredericks.

Tom Fredericks was a true countryman and would make ladders for fruit picking, one of which I still have today. Tom would also cut your hair in his tarred hut, selling bedding plants there too. He was a keen gardener, up at first light in the summer months to tend his plants. When I used to visit Tom with my father, I had the job to turn his old grindstone so he could sharpen his knives and so on. Tom started work on the canal in 1935. He retired in the late 1960s and went to live with his sister in Gloucester. But after a life in the peace of the country he never went on long. He was brought home to Hardwicke after he died where he lies at rest in the churchyard.

Richard Cale
(b. 1943)

Mr W.L. Ives, Assistant General Manager, presents the prize to Ivor Prosser and his family for their award-winning garden.

The day the canal sprung a leak.

Award-winning garden

As well as operating the bridge for the various craft it was also my responsibility to carry out routine maintenance, paint the bridge every year and keep the surrounding banks and hedges trimmed and tidy. I always took pride in my very large garden and with the help of my wife and two daughters the hard work paid off when we won the Richie Trophy for the Best Kept Bridge, Lock and Gardens for the whole of British Waterways – something we were very proud of.

Ivor Prosser
(b. 1919)

Canal froze over

The 1962-63 winter caused the canal to freeze over, with ice two and three inches thick. The bridgeman at The Pilot, Ivor Prosser, walked across it. In fact the ice was so severe that, further down at Framilode, people actually walked across the river. To keep the canal open, as in those days commercial traffic was still important up and down the canal, tugs *Mayflower* and *Primrose* kept the waterway open and cleared a path for boats bringing grain and timber to the timber yards of Nicks and Griggs. Here the boats coming up from Sharpness Docks would be unloaded by men running up and down the unloading planks at piecework rates. Rough chocolate was also brought up on boats, up to the Cadbury's factory at Frampton and then onto Cadbury's at Bourneville. Often packets would break open and some of our school friends from Frampton would bring it up to Quedgeley School. What a great taste it was – I shall remember it for as long as I live.

Richard Cale
(b. 1943)

Bad winters

We had some bad winters here, they had to get men to come and dig the bridge out. They had icebreakers going up and down the canal day and night. It got so bad that one day a tanker stopped at the bridge and a man on the boat asked me to get some fags from the pub for him - I walked out to the boat to hand them over. Our youngest was born in the very bad winter of 1946-7. The passmen couldn't ride the banks so they had to come and stay with us all day.

Ivor Prosser
(b. 1919)

An empty canal

In 1990 a culvert under the canal broke further up from Quedgeley at the Castle Bridge, which led to the water draining out. Hundreds of people came to see. I myself walked along the bottom of the cut. It was a sight I'll probably never seen again in my lifetime.

Richard Cale
(b. 1943)

The disappearing cat

Our cabin was situated on the same side of the canal as The Pilot pub, about 100 yards further south. There were several other similar cabins on the same stretch. I noticed while visiting The Pilot a couple of years back that they had all disappeared, although the more substantial buildings on the opposite side of the canal, the other side of the bridge, remain. These were real homes. On what was then the main road, before the bypass was built, was a small bakers shop and we bought from there delicious loaves which were still steaming hot! On one visit my parents decided to take our cat. Blackie was duly placed in the basket on the front of mother's bicycle and spent the weekend with us. The problem came when it was time to go home on the Sunday afternoon - Blackie was nowhere to be found. He had obviously taken to the countryside as enthusiastically as me and had gone walkabout. We returned home without

The Bridge House at Sellars Bridge in 1945.

Hardwicke Bridge House, shortly before restoration work began in 1993.

the wandering moggy. The next weekend we returned to the cabin. Blackie was found but the gentle, domesticated creature we had known had transformed into a wild, spitting minx. I suppose fending for himself in that natural, rural world was totally beyond his experience as a town cat.

Mike Sheridan

Capsizing boats

When we first moved to our Bridge House on the canal I was scared of the water. We had a little boat for going backwards and forwards, across where the bridge would have been, but I didn't like going in it – I thought the boat would sink and we would all drown. I liked watching the boats though; one day a tall ship came past – it had been used in a programme on the television, and was coming down from Gloucester docks. It really was an amazing sight because it was so big. Our house is quite famous – we've been on the television too. A man called Quentin Willson came with a film crew to make a programme called *All The Right Moves*. It was about unusual homes, and they filmed us in our house, and then they all went out in our boat to film the canal.

The tall ships are a magnificent sight on the canal.

They spent all day at our house, but the bit they showed on the television was only a few minutes long. Our house has also been featured in lots of magazines and newspapers. People think it's interesting because you get to it by boat or by walking across fields, instead of by car. One day a photographer came to take a picture of it, and he thought it would be good if he took the photograph from the middle of the canal, looking up at the house. So he got into our little boat but unfortunately he made it tip up, and he fell in with a big splash. He was soaked, and he cut his arm on the rocks in the canal, but luckily he had given his camera to my mum to hold as he got in, so that was saved. He was very relieved about that. He went home and another photographer came the next day – he took the picture from the opposite bank.

I also fell into the canal when my rowing boat capsized. I stopped being frightened of the water and joined the Rowing Club and one day, when we hadn't been going for very long, we managed to tip our boat over and five of us fell in. But we had been taught what to do if that happened and I wasn't scared. I love rowing; it's great fun.

Portia Ashenford
(b. 1990)

A tall ship makes its way up the canal.

Television presenter Quentin Wilson and crew during the filming of a BBC programme about Hardwicke Bridge House.

7 During the War

Married in haste

My grandparents, Frank and Clara Driver, moved to Llanwern, Sellars Road in Hardwicke in 1929 or 1930. They had four children: Arthur and Dora were already married and had left home, and Phyllis (my mother) and Peter were still at home. My mother was fifteen years old when the family arrived. My grandparents ran the local shop and post office and my mother, after leaving school, helped run the shop. Her younger brother Peter was very clever with electrics and won gold medals for his endeavours. My father, William Willis, lived at Panholme on the Bath Road in Hardwicke, near the Cross Keys, with his mother and sister. He worked for the Electricity Board. Phyllis and William courted and were betrothed to be married on 3 September 1939. Unfortunately Hitler had other ideas and the wedding took place in great haste at Hardwicke church two days earlier, on 1 September 1939. My father then left immediately for the war. He was a soldier in the Royal Artillery. Peter Driver joined the RAF and gave his life. He is remembered at the War Memorial in the Lychgate of Hardwicke church. After the war my father returned to work with the Electricity Board – he was the time clerk for the Central Electricity Generating Board at Castle Meads. He was also a Special Sergeant in the Gloucestershire Constabulary.

Anne Hocking (née Willis)
(b. 1947)

Land army life

When I went in the Land Army I learned a lot. I was taught how to bottle fruit and kill and draw a chicken – which I thought I would never do in my life. I learned a lot off Mrs Merrett at Whitminster. There were two of us at first when we did our training. Then the other girl went on to Slimbridge. Next door to where the nursing home is was a big house, and a Welsh farmer lived there so when I left the Land Army to have my little boy I used to help him with his apples and cows, and his washing and cooking. He used to take the stool out and milk the cows in the field. His name was Mr Williams, Dave Williams. He used to let rooms to the girls who worked in the offices around Quedgeley. He had about four girls living in his house. They worked for the RAF, doing clerical work.

Marjorie Dobbs
(b. 1916)

Air-raid shelter

There was an air raid shelter on the canal bank, near the bridge, and if the air raid warning went off while we were at school, we had to go back there. If the warning went off we were all sent to individual places, and John and I had to come back to this little steel hut on the side of the bank that the bridgeman – Tom Fredricks – had. I always thought we would be far worse off in the shelter than we would have been outside – we would get blown straight into the canal.

Eric Vick (b. 1929)

The air raids

My husband used to go off to work at 7.30 in the morning and not come home until 7.30 at night. So I used to put my little boy in the pram and take our dinner round to the canal, and I used to read and sew and knit. My husband used to be called out just about every night; he was an emergency linesman. So when the air raids came I used to sit on the stairs nursing my little boy. When my Dad found out he said 'None of that, you come into Gloucester' so after that I used to go into Gloucester.

Marjorie Dobbs
(b. 1916)

Village postman Vic Charles served in the Navy during the war.

Vic Charles and family.

A lucky escape

In 1941 we had living with us an uncle and aunt, who were refugees from Belgium. My uncle, in the First World War, went to Belgium and married. He was a groom for polo ponies. He married a lady out there, and they came to us when Belgium was invaded. He worked at the 7MU. One day he was sitting in the back bedroom, putting his clothes on, and he saw this plane, and he saw the bombs drop – several in a row. One dropped in the centre of the Bristol Road, right outside our house.

We were three girls, all sharing a room, in a bed with an iron bedstead. The roof came in and if it hadn't been for the iron bedstead the roof trusses would have been on us and we would have been injured.

So we went walking along the little corridor

to my mum's bedroom – we managed to struggle along there over all the debris – and went in. Mum and Dad were just looking around and the first thing mum said was 'Open the window, Jack'. But there wasn't a pane of glass in there. Fortunately no-one was seriously injured. Dad was a member of the ARP, so he was busy outside. A little while later Miss Lloyd-Baker came along – she was in charge of the ARP – and she said, 'Wyer, why haven't you got your tin hat on?' And he said: 'Tin hat be ★★★★★★★★. I haven't got a roof on my house!'

Evelyn Sims
(b. 1923)

Slept through the bombs

There was a bomb which hit the canal bank which blew the bank out, and another by the farmhouse (School Farm) which blew the ceiling down. My brother and I were in bed downstairs and the ceiling fell on him, and he never even woke up. The plaster ceiling came down and covered him, but he just slept on. There were seven bombs in a line, which killed some sheep.

Eric Vick
(b. 1929)

Blacksmith Jack Wyer enjoys a relaxing moment. His home was struck by a bomb during the war.

Jack Wyer engrossed in a game of Shove Ha'penny

Allotment surprise

During the war they dropped a string of bombs over Hardwicke. One fell on the allotments, in Charlie Smith's allotment, one demolished a cottage near the blacksmith's shop. It did a lot of damage, but no-one was seriously hurt.

John Drinkwater
(b. 1915)

A frightening time

I was hanging the clothes out one Monday morning and a plane came over and dropped its bomb at Hardwicke. We could see the markings on its side. It was very frightening, the war. When the Yanks started coming, it was tanks and lorries. My little boy used to stand on the gate and they would throw him sweets and chewing gum. They would go down the Bristol Road, going down to the coast I suppose. Hundreds and hundreds of them. You could hear them rattling by at night as well.

Marjorie Dobbs
(b. 1916)

8 Leisure Time and Celebration

A fete held at Hardwicke Court in 1936/37.

The rifle club

There was a rifle club in Hardwicke when I was a child and that was built on the south end of the school. The rifle club used to meet about once a month. They used to move all the benches and desks back, put mattresses down at one end and fire through the school, through the doorway into targets fixed to a big box filled with earth. At the back of the box was a steel plate to stop the bullets.

Charlie Smith

Magic lantern shows

Opposite our cottage was a small conifer plantation. The large green area halfway along Green Lane, near the pond, was used by Romany Gypsies, with their colourful horse-drawn vans, as a stop-over during their journeys to and from the Herefordshire hop fields. They and their animals used our well for their water supply. We found them to be good folk, well behaved and tidy. In the late forties the green was also the meeting place for the local hunt and I used to take the children to see the men in their red coats and the horses and dogs. In the old village hall they

Hardwicke Court was again the venue for a village fete – this time in 2001.

used to hold magic lantern shows of holiday photographs.

Cherry Stack

An annual treat

The children had a school treat each year. We used to meet at the school and every child had his cup and we used to march from school down the back way, to Hardwicke Court, flags and Union Jacks flying and all that. We sang all the way down and then the old Squire came out and spoke to us, hoping we would have a nice, pleasant, afternoon. Oh yes, it was very nice and very rural and the children thought a lot of it in those days because it was the only pleasure they got. We had our tea on the terrace in front of the house, sitting on benches at long tables. We were given Chelsea buns, other buns, and blackberry jam which were accompanied by a liberal supply of wasps. There used to be as many wasps as we had jam. Some of the men from the Court Estate, Mr Walter Franklin and Mr Ted Woodman, would go out into Hardwicke Court Park and put up swings from the oak trees, and there was a nicely mowed cricket pitch as well. After the tea the children used to have races - they ran 100yds for about 2d old money.

Charlie Smith

Our own entertainment

We made our entertainment, there was no TV, not even any electricity. Light came from oil lamps, then gas lamps until finally electricity arrived with us in the early 1950s. Even then the road was not lit until 1969.

The radio was a main source of entertainment. Radio Luxembourg is a station I eagerly looked forward to along with my

Hardwicke Court was again the venue for a village fete – this time in 2001.

Eagle comic. For entertainment father would attend the weekly whist drives in the village hall, a tradition he kept up until he died. Sometimes on a Friday evening in the late 1940s and early 1950s Mr Gage, a showman, would put film shows on for us in the village hall. He was a respected man and when he died showmen from all over the country came to pay their respects. It was one of the largest funerals I can ever recall at Quedgeley church. His resting place can be found in the churchyard near the Curtis Hayward vault.

Richard Cale
(b. 1943)

No stilettos

The present Quedgeley village hall was built in 1962 at a cost of £9,000 and was opened by Miles Curtis Hayward. As villagers we were invited to come and attend the opening. However the invitation came with a condition! Young men were permitted to wear their 'winkle pickers' – fashionable at the time – but the ladies were forbidden to wear stilettos as they were seen to damage the wooden flooring inside. The new village hall was a replacement of the original hall that burned down in the late 1950s.

Richard Cale
(b. 1943)

Fox hunts

I also remember the fox hunts that took place from Hardwicke Court. One day all the riders, horses and dogs stopped out in the field alongside Springfield and we all had a good view of this quite regular occasion.

One day, in that same field, an aeroplane

fuel tank crash landed, just missing the house where I now live. We thought it great excitement and crowds soon gathered around to get a good look.

Mary Sims

Quedgeley village hall

Quedgeley Village Hall had whist drives and dances. You would also take the babies there to be weighed, get your vitamins and fruit juice and so on. There wasn't much social life, mainly we used to listen to the radio and play cards.

Bettina Brewis
(b. 1922)

Whist drives and dances

Hardwicke was quite a community on its own, but it had to find its own pleasure. And people did, we used to have whist drives and dances at Hardwicke s chool. Half a crown for a whist drive and dance, including refreshments - ham sandwiches, tea, coffee or lemonade. About four fellows, one on the piano, one on drums, one with a violin and another with a trumpet - cornet - used to come up from Stroud.

Charlie Smith

The Queen's Coronation

I moved from Moreton Valence Camp to Springfield in the last week of May 1953. It was the year of the Queen's Coronation and a lot of activity was taking place in Springfield. There was a big marquee on the round green up by the grey houses. As we were the only tenants in the brown houses the neighbours from the grey houses attached a row of flags to the guttering of our roof, at No. 19, so we too were included in the celebrations. This was

A busy stall at the 2001 village fete.

kindly and expertly done by Mrs Screen and Mr and Mrs Laugharne. All the children had a sit down party inside the tent and we also had fun and games with a race from the green to the telephone box. I can't remember who won or what the first prize was. Each child was given a Coronation mug and a pencil box with a picture of the Queen and Prince Philip on the front. The jelly and trifles were the best we ever tasted.

Mary Sims

Church choir outing

In the summer we were taken for the Hardwicke church choir outing to Weston or Cheddar. They used to get a box, a nice little box, and buy a cooked ham and so many loaves and my mother and one or two helpers used to come to my home and cut up sandwiches and fill this box, for the boys' dinner when they

Around the fountain at Hardwicke Court.

got to Weston. Some cycled and others went on a trolley provided by Mr Michael Lloyd-Baker, Miss Olive Lloyd-Baker's father, driven by Arthur Chandler, to take us up to the station to get the train. Mr Risbey got on in Gloucester and met us at Haresfield. On the way down every boy was given one shilling or one and six to spend. Some of them that had decent homes and could afford it got half a crown from their parents. But, bless me, one boy was found with two or three shillings in his pocket, he got two or three boys to help him spend it during the day. He was the banker, the moneyed man of the party.

Sometimes we sat down under the sea wall, or on the beach, with a jar of cider - we took ten quarts of lemonade and some cider with us - and have our dinner. Then the boys were let loose, but they'd got to be back at a certain place for afternoon tea. Then we made our way back to the railways station and took the train back to Haresfield, then we had to walk home from there in those days because Arthur Chandler didn't come out in the evening.

Charlie Smith

Carol singing

A lot of the village children would go carol singing at Christmas with lovely lanterns, and we would go round the Quedgeley singing carols.

Valerie Hodges
(b. 1943)

Friendly dances

As for social life, that involved riding your bike around the village to see if there were any girls around. That was about the extent of it. The GFS, (Girls' Friendly Society) used to hold dances at Hardwicke school, and I was often roped in to being the doorman. It was about one and sixpence in those days, to come in. We had a few whist drives and beetle drives, but nothing much.

Eric Vick
(b. 1929)

Cricket match

Miss Olive Lloyd-Baker used to have a cricket match in front of the court every year. My Dad used to go down and play. I can remember them playing a game in front of the Cross Keys on the little triangular piece of ground in front of the pub. They played with broad shovels.

Eric Vick

Fined for no lights

My dad used to go to The Pilot every night, and you could set your watch by him. He would go at half past eight and come back spot on ten o'clock. I can remember seeing him every night getting his carbine lamp ready. It would be attached by a bracket to the front of his bike. One night it caught fire and he came home with no lights, and the local policeman had him. He had to go to Whitminster court for no lights and he was fined, I think, five shillings. I don't suppose anyone now would know how to light a carbine lamp – it was a work of art.

Eric Vick
(b. 1929)

Church bellringers

My grandfather and father were bellringers at Hardwicke church, and I did a lot of ringing.

There was old Charles Parsons, a relation of my wife's, wonderful old man he was, big, stout, man, and, do you know, that old man could ring with his eyes shut. He'd often go on like that and he'd catch the sally [the thickened end of the bell-rope], he'd put his hands up and catch the sally just like that. I've often seen him ring for a couple of minutes with his eyes shut. Then there was Bert Selwyn, he was the carpenter down at the Elm for Mr Lloyd-Baker, Ted Sims, Bert Nash, my father and myself. In those days we used to have a ringers' supper. Mr Stowell was at Church Farm and he was a very, very good gentleman and he always supplied the meat for the supper. It was held in the village school and he would come up just after Christmas and see my father in his boot shop and he'd say: 'Well, isn't it time we had a get together with the ringers, getting time isn't it?' Father would say: 'Yes, you'd better get your book out and see how many there are'. There would be the ringers, two or three farmer friends, the churchwardens and some others. We'd get the money together for beer, they had nine gallons of beer and ten quarts of cider, mixed pickles, beetroots, bread and cheese, tobacco and cigarettes. The meat was cooked at my house and it was my job to help mother cook it. It was sent down from the butcher's in Gloucester, from Alfred Warner's, salt beef, 25lbs in one piece with a big piece of fat on the top. It was delivered to our house and father used to get a strong cord and tie it round the meat, with a loop at the top so that you could pick it up. We used to put the furnace on, and when the furnace boiled father and I would pick the meat up by the loop and put it into the boiling water, mother took the time it was put in. It stayed in there and simmered all day long, until 8 or 9pm. It was my job to keep that water boiling, it wasn't to go off the boil. Then it was put on a big meat dish in the scullery and allowed to cool for the supper the following night.

Hardwicke school May Day celebrations.

More May Day celebrations.

The beer was delivered by the brewery at Church House and father and I took the rest down in the truck, pushed it down to the school. The children had a half-day off and the desks were pushed back and we had tables and benches from the Court set up down the middle of the school. We had tableclothes and father and I spent the afternoon laying up the tables and getting everything ready. Then we'd lock the school, come home and have a bit of tea ourselves and then get off back to the school. The bellringers would know what time to get there and they'd go over to the church and have a turn of ringing. They'd ring for perhaps half an hour. Then we would go and get Mr Stowell, he always came and carved, dressed very nicely in his big coat, nice white shirt with a bow tie, breeches and cloth leggings, he was a big hefty man. Every man's plate was full of beef, a big slashing of meat, and they helped themselves to beer which was put on the tables in jugs. They had a thoroughly good supper. Then they would go back to the church again and have another

little touch of ringing and then lower the bells and come back.

The school was lit by paraffin lamps in those days and we had a good fire burning in the grate. We used to draw the piano up by the fire, the late Mr Harold Lyes used to be our pianist, and we sang all sorts of songs and different things interspersed with a few hymns or something of that. Anyway, we had a jolly good evening and finished up about half past midnight or 1.00 a.m. Then we would clear the tables and take the benches outside to leave the school empty for the cleaners to come in the next day. Father and I had to put all the remains back into the truck and push it home at about 1.30 in the morning. The meat that was left was cut up and used in sandwiches.

The men used to assemble again at the church to ring the Old Year out and the New Year in. I had to go over to Hardwicke Farm, Tom Webb lived there then, taking a ten quart jar and have it filled and then take it back to the church. There's been many and many a ten quart jar put in that old stoke-hole in the back of the church and locked up. We used to eat the sandwiches, either in the school or in the stoke-hole, and then get on with the ringing. Old Charles Parsons, he was very particular over how the bells rang. If there was a young one that had got out of place and came down a bit before the others and clashed with him he would shout: 'Kip 'em right, kip 'em steady - them got iron tongues, you can hear them all over the parish'. Oh yes, he'd jump on a young 'un.

Charlie Smith

Pony and trap

Every year Miss Clare Lloyd-Baker, Miss Olive's aunt, used to take five or six of us at a time in her pony and trap up to Haresfield Beacon as a treat. Then every year we used to have a fete in front of Hardwicke Court, with children racing and so on. In the big trees there were swings – it was always a lovely day out.

John Drinkwater
(b. 1915)

Hardwicke and district choir

The debut of the Hardwicke and District Choir, under its conductor Mr W. Smith of Mostyn, Hardwicke, was a resounding success both socially and financially. The choir were guest entertainers at a musical evening held at Haresfield Court (by kind permission of Mrs T. Heywood) in aid of the South Gloucester Deanery Association for Social Work, and entertained the assembled company with selections of light music both before and after supper. The informal atmosphere of the whole

Hardwicke football team.

Miss Olive Lloyd-Baker entertained the children of the parish to a Coronation tea.

evening was greatly enhanced by the gracious house in which it was held.

Thanking the singers, Mrs Heywood congratulated them and said the Three Choirs would need to look to their laurels, as the newly formed Hardwicke Choir of thirty voices would present a real challenge. One hundred and fifty people spent a delightful evening and the money raised will be most useful for the Gloucester Diocesan Social Work Committee.

From The Citizen, *October 1975*

The village celebrated the coronation with a carnival and fancy dress competition. Pictured are Kathleen Fredericks (left) and William Willis.

The village was again in celebratory mood for the Queen's Silver Jubilee with a carnival and games. This is the Village Hall float.

Games galore

We moved into Springfield in 1950, as soon as the house was built, and the hall had a stone floor that we painted green. If I had promised a picnic and the weather was too wet we would lay blankets on this side of the hall floor and arrange the children's toy farm animals on one side, like a farm in the distance, and have our picnic there instead.

Their dad made them a playground with a roundabout made from an old round table, a swing from railway sleepers and other bits and a seesaw from an old concrete roller. We had lots of little animals; dogs, cats, guinea pigs, mice, one boy used to go about with a slow-worm in his pocket. A budgie in a cage used to hang up there, by the window, and we even had a hedgehog. It was like a little farm here, it was wonderful!

Since I knew what it was like to go without real food when I was young, before being put into the orphanage, sometimes for three or four days, I joined a club that sold food hampers all through the year. Using that I would build up my food stocks. As a special treat I'd put the girls in one room and the boys and their friends under the stairs and give them each a tin opener and a couple of spoons and a hamper to work their way through. They had a wonderful time. We had races and games in the front garden, which was all lawn then. I would have a collection of penny chews and other small prizes, and it was always 'arranged' that every child got a prize for something.

At Christmas we used to do different things with the presents. My husband and I would spend a long time tearing up newspaper to put into a barrel to make a sort of bran tub. Then we would put all the presents in the tub and play Hunt-the-Thimble. Whoever found the thimble could take a present out of the tub. It might not be their present so they had to hand it over, but this way they each got their presents all through the day instead of all at once in the morning. One time their father dressed up as Father Christmas and we had the kiddies in a row. We thought his disguise was wonderful, but the youngest one kept looking: 'That's our Dad, he's got our Dad's shoes on!' Another year we would hide the presents all over the house and they would be finding them for days. Once we gave them each a huge parcel, but that was made up of lots of little parcels. My husband used to make up lots of games for the children to play, and we always gave him a booby-present, something small wrapped up in lots and lots of paper. We had to buy those presents all through the year, we couldn't afford a big expense all at once. They might have missed out on other things, but we always made sure they all had a good birthday and Christmas. I used to start making Christmas cakes early, first little ones and then bigger and bigger ones until the final iced one for Christmas Day. The excuse was that they could eat the little ones first to get their stomachs used to rich food ready for Christmas!

Cherry Stack

A terrible dance floor

There wasn't much of a social life. I belonged to the Scouts. Miss Peggy Jones, Miss Olive Lloyd–Baker's companion, used to run the Scouts and we used the Reformatory. We also used the outbuildings at Hardwicke Court, and we had a canoe on the lake there. There were also village dances at Hardwicke School – the floor was terrible, they used to sprinkle something on it so we could dance. You could only get about fifteen people on the dance floor. Everyone used to muck in and move the seats. There used to be a little band – Edgar Chamberlain played the drums, I can't remember who played the piano. But that was it – just piano and drums. But it was very enjoyable.

John Drinkwater
(b. 1915)

Never bored

Swimming was a favourite pastime. No Leisure Centres in my youth, only the old Gloucester Baths in Eastgate Street, Cheltenham Lido or Stratford Park in Stroud. We'd also swim in the canal, often cutting our feet on the barnacles. The word 'bored' never entered my vocabulary!

Later in my youth I also played football for the Hardwicke AFC – for nearly twenty seasons – and in the long summer days, cricket for Elmore.

Apart from swimming in the canal, we'd fish there too, catching many a bootlace near the Pilot Bridge.

Richard Cale
(b. 1943)

Youth groups

I was a member of the Band of Hope in them days. We met at the church. And they used to have what they called the Junior

The crowds gather for the Silver Jubilee celebrations.

Caroline Bell (centre) was the Silver Jubilee princess.

Hardwicke WI members plant a tree on the Green in 1974.

Imperial League, and that was run, I think, at Quedgeley Village Hall. I think the girls used to go there, my sister used to go there and there was a Girls' Friendly Society - the GFS they called it.

Ivor Prosser
(b. 1919)

Jubilee celebrations

The clerk reported he had received a circular letter from the Ministry of Health authorising parish councils to raise a rate for the Jubilee celebrations. Mr Williams said he didn't think the idea of a rate would be very well received generally. The clerk said he had had a conversation with the chairman, Miss Lloyd-Baker, who said she would give the same as the Squire did in 1911, namely, give the children a tea at Hardwicke Court and subscribe £2 to a fund for providing a tea for adults, and sports. Mr Smith said after the chairman's generous offer he didn't think there would be any difficulty in raising sufficient funds to provide tea and sports and he would propose that when the council next met the old Parish Tea Committee be asked to attend and to make what arrangements were necessary. Mr Williams seconded. Carried.

From the Minutes of Hardwicke Parish Council
27 February 1935

Coronation mugs

Another monumental occasion was the Coronation in 1953. The children at Hardwicke school received mugs and Bibles. The village was in carnival mood and everyone took part in fancy dress.

Anne Hocking (née Willis)
(b. 1947)

Stuntman Dick Sheppard joined WI ladies on a sponsored walk.

Hardwicke WI's twenty-fifth anniversary party.

9 Down on the Farm

Horses played a large part in farm life. The boy in the picture is contributor Geoff Martin.

On the milk run

I used to work for the Milk Marketing Board until I retired about nine years ago. I worked there for about twenty years, sometimes doing long runs, taking milk all over the country, and sometimes I did the farm collections in the smaller lorries, picking up milk from local farms. One of the runs included about five farms in Hardwicke and several in the villages around about. Hardwicke Court farm produced a colossal amount of milk, probably about 2,000 litres. The milk would be collected from the farms once a day, mornings mostly, although those at the end of the run

wouldn't be picked up until after lunch. So that would be the evening before's milking as well as that morning's.

One thing that definitely improved over the twenty years I was doing the run was the hygiene on the farms. That got a lot better. There was one farm in Hardwicke where it was really clean, but some of them, when I started the run, left a lot to be desired.

It's very difficult for dairy farmers now. They are struggling because they're not getting the price for their milk. They've got to feed the cows and take care of them, and it's costing more to produce the milk than to sell it.

The Vaughn family from Hardwicke at work with the tractor.

Of course the big estates weren't there in Hardwicke then, although there was a lot of housing in Quedgeley even then. But the farmers were always very friendly, they would always say 'Good morning' and have a little chat. There were always plenty of friendly farm dogs too. Many of the farms had been handed down from father to son.

The farms varied enormously in size. You would go into one farm and collect fifty or eighty litres of milk, and then in the next one it could be two or three thousand litres.

Before they built the creamery at Stonehouse, all the milk collected from the local farms would be pumped into big tankers and could be sent all over the country. The runs I did included London, Wales and Cambridge. One of my most frequent trips was to Llangadog in Wales where milk was taken to the Co-op creamery and turned into rice pudding. Some of the milk was taken to other places and turned into milk powder.

Even when they built the creamery, some milk was still transported to other places. You never knew from one day to the next where you would be going, because one place might have too much milk so you would be sent somewhere else. It certainly made the job interesting.

But many years before I began working for the Milk Marketing Board, back in the 1960s, I used to collect milk for Severn Valley Dairies, based in Stonehouse. Mr and Mrs Hudson had it. The milk was collected from local farms, and we had to dip a special piece of paper in it – if the paper changed colour it was fine, if not we had to reject it. The milk was then collected in churns, and it was taken to the dairy, pasteurised and bottled. Any surplus milk was taken to the Cadbury factory in Frampton. The bottled milk was then delivered on the milk round - so it was local milk going to local people.

Don Underwood (b. 1929)

Farming is still a big part of life in Hardwicke.

Chickens were much more common on the mixed farms in Quedgeley and hardwicke twenty-five years ago. Now they are kept mainly as pets.

Quedgeley House

My grandfather had a farm at Elmore, but when my father first got married he moved out of the farm and my parents lived in Quedgeley House, which had been converted into flats. It was owned by the Moreland family then, and it was cheap, rented accommodation.

From there they set up in business with my uncle, and they worked as farming contractors around this area. They had one of the first balers around this area, and before the baling they started off with the threshing, and then the combining. They did a fair bit of contracting, covering a big area, from here to Hempsted to Hucclecote, all round Tuffley. This was in the 1960s.

When I started going out with Linda, who's now my wife, I took her to see Quedgeley House, so she could see where I grew up. But when we got there it had gone! It was knocked down in about 1982, or '83, and the bricks were used for a grain store at Epney.

Graham Lovell (b. 1960)

This little piggy...

One cold winter morning when I was doing the run, collecting milk from the farms, the farmer said to me: 'Come on in, Don, and have a cup of tea and get yourself warm.' So we went into the farm kitchen, which was lovely and warm, and we were sitting at the table having a cup of tea. This farmer had pigs as well as cows and one of the pigs had had a litter during the night. But the smallest pig of the litter, the runt, wasn't doing very well at all, so they had brought him in to keep him warm. There was an old-fashioned range in this kitchen, an Aga, or something like it, and the little piggy was in a cardboard box on top of this Aga, keeping warm. The farmer and I were chatting away when suddenly there was a whooshing noise and I turned round to see the cardboard box going up in flames! Fortunately the little pig was unhurt – definitely a case of the farmer saving his bacon!

Don Underwood (b. 1929)

Different cattle

Quedgeley in those days, back when I was growing up in the '60s and '70s, was just great big open fields of rough pasture and grazing, oak tress, a few fruit trees, rough hedges, ponds – tadpoles and everything. It was really quite rough and overgrown; it wasn't farmed to any intensity at all. It was grazed by big Hereford cattle – you don't see many of those around any more. They are brown with a white face, and when they are crossed with the Friesians they are black and white, but with the Hereford features. You would see a lot of the short-horn crosses too.

If you were in no rush to finish them for fattening, you could keep a Hereford bullock for four years. You can't do that now, of course, since BSE – you've got to finish your cattle before they are two and half years old. So you can't just let them roam to fatten in whatever time they need. You've got to push them on and get them finished before they are two and a half years old, which intensifies farming.

The dairy cows now are bred to produce a lot of milk, so the cows are bigger and taller, completely different to the old British breeds. In the sixties you would have more of a dual purpose breed that was a bit beefy, would produce enough milk, but would also produce a good calf that would then produce your good beef.

The old bull used to be taken from farm to

Today many of the farms – such as Waterwells Farm – have vanished. This is now a business park and the base for the Quedgeley Park and Ride.

The area's farming heritage lives on in the names of the local roads.

Once a field - now a housing estate.

farm – that's not allowed now either, but it used to happen in the 1960s. At Haywick Farm, they took a bull there once, and they couldn't get him back loaded again!

Cattle would be slaughtered locally too – there was an abattoir, Baxter's, behind where the Kentucky Fried Chicken place is now, so meat would be bred, slaughtered, sold and eaten locally. In fact, our 'pet' cow was slaughtered and came back to us ready for the freezer – my sister was so upset, she's never eaten meat since!

Graham Lovell (b. 1960)

The motorway arrives

When they were building the motorway, we went for a walk down there and pushed the kids in their pram down the middle of the road. It was just before they put the hard stuff down. We walked down because we knew we wouldn't get a chance to do something like that again. It was a big development for the area – to think the motorway was going right next to us. Some people were excited, but not everyone was pleased.

I remember these men boring holes one day, to see what the sub soil was, and I asked my uncle what they were doing. He said: 'Oh it's for that road. They did it all once before, before the war. It'll never come.'

Apparently they marked it all out before the war, with concrete markers. It was a slightly different route then. The link road was going to go through a little school farm that I had, and there were concrete markers. There was one stuck in the middle of the courtyard – I expect it's still there.

In those days all the Midlands traffic had to go over Gloucester cross. The A38 went straight through the middle of Gloucester. It was a very busy road – at times the traffic could be terrible.

Geoff Martin (b. 1938)

Honest toil

Hardwicke reformatory was built in 1852, and it was sited in the middle of farmland well away from the villagers. It was founded by Thomas Barwick Lloyd Baker for the juvenile 'delinquents' of the day, because he felt an alternative to prison life was needed for these young offenders so that they could have a chance to 'reform' and lead useful lives.

There is a great deal of information available on the reformatory because excellent records were kept. A file on the boys admitted to the reformatory in 1868 reveals that they came from Cheltenham, Malmesbury, Stroud and even Stafford. They were aged between ten and eighteen, serving sentences ranging from two years to five years, their crimes mainly stealing and pick-pocketing.

As with many of the Quedgeley estates, this one gives a clue to its previous existence.

Field Court Farm once existed near by this road.

They had to work on the farm under the strict supervision of Mr Robinson, a very hard taskmaster, and a couple of equally strict masters, who lived in the cottage across the field.

Mr Lloyd Baker liked them to dig 'the blue clay of Hardwicke' because it left the hands calloused and blistered – and not at all suitable to the pickpocket's trade. It also meant that they became fit and strong and would be an asset to any farmer who might wish to employ them in the future. Many boys did go on to work on local farms, and would be apprenticed for five years. Others, no doubt inspired by the boats they saw daily on the canal, emigrated to Canada and the USA, joined the army or went to sea.

Corporal punishment – usually birching – was common at the reformatory; the records show that in 1886 'boy Dangerfield was reported for stealing a bushel of apples from the orchard' and 'a good birching' was ordered.

Behind the main building, heated by coal which the boys would have to unload from the wharf at the canal and haul some 600 yards across the fields to the school, was a second smaller building, used as a laundry. Everything was washed by hand and put through wooden mangles. Upstairs was the ironing room.

But as well as harsh manual tasks, the boys played football and cricket, and were given lessons in composition and mental arithmetic, history, geography and other subjects. Many found steady employment after leaving the school.

The main reformatory building has been demolished, but the laundry is still there, and so is School Farm.

David Kear

School project

There was a farmer in Quedgeley called Mr Phipps, and his wife was a teacher at Quedgeley Primary school. Every week when I was a pupil there we went along to the farm to do our little projects on the farm. We used to walk round the fields and pace it out and then try to work out the acreage, and all things like that. We did that once a week – it never felt like work, but we were learning maths and such like. The new bypass cut right through his drive and he has now got a bridge underneath.

The school is where the youth centre is now. It used to be two classrooms right up against the road, then a big assembly hall, then there were another three classrooms. It was a big school for the area, with over 100 pupils. We had an art room and a music room. There was a canteen with cooking done on the site and taken to all the other little local schools like Elmore and Longney. A lot of pupils came from Naas Lane, RAF families.

Graham Lovell (b. 1960)

A vet's life

I started in practice as a vet back in the mid-1960s in Gloucester, and I worked in Stroud for a while. I came here having worked abroad for a bit, in Africa. It wasn't quite as primitive in rural Gloucestershire as in Africa – but in places it was certainly fairly basic.

Cattle have changed a good deal since those days – it tends to be just the black and white now. They had an enormous selection of cows and Old Gloucester's down at Wick Court in Arlingham. We used to look after the cattle there for the Miss Dowdeswells. They were very quaint, practically Victorian. They had no electricity or running water, with toilets over the moat in three different sizes, so the family could all sit down together! They had the last commercial herd of Old Gloucester's in the country.

But the old-fashioned farms have disappeared, with the farmyard with the chickens running round and the pigs round the back. The old country traditions are dying. They wasted

A master and boys at the Reformatory.

Boys at work in the classroom at Hardwicke Reformatory.

nothing in the country in the old days – everybody had a few pigs and chickens and the waste food from the house was always fed to the chickens or the pigs. Nothing was wasted, and everything was valued. Things were much easier in those days in many ways, without regulations, and people could get on and live their lives without too much interference from government. Even in the town of Gloucester you would be surprised how many people kept pigs, just round the back of their houses, or on little allotment areas. There were lots of slaughterhouses in villages, and people would salt the pigs down on slabs and make their own bacon. That's all disappeared now.

It was a bit like something from *All Creatures Great and Small* in those days. I can remember being on a farm one day and the farmer was there with an excruciatingly agonised expression. He had terrible, terrible toothache. He showed me his tooth and it was very wobbly and his gums were very swollen. He asked me to take it out, so I agreed. He just hung onto this beam and I found a pair of tweezers from the car and took it out. He was very, very grateful. I asked 'Did you feel any pain from that?' and he said 'No, all I felt was relief!'

Just in the short time I've been in practice there have been enormous changes in agriculture. A lot of farms had three generations working alongside each other on the farm. Grampy would still be active, and his son, and the grandchildren would help too. They would expect to spend their life on the farm. These days the young people aren't interested. The money isn't there, for one thing, and it's a lot of hard work, and that way of life doesn't appeal to them any more.

Dairy herds were much smaller when I started. A farmer could make a living from twenty or thirty cows. Hand-milking might take place before school, with mum, dad and a couple of children all helping before they went to school. There's no chance of making a living now from that size herd.

Bill Stewart (b. 1940)

Local markets for local food

The corn used to be hauled up to Pridays at Gloucester. It would come straight off the field and onto the wagon and up to Pridays. But you had to get up there early in the morning, say four or five o' clock in the morning, because everyone was up there queuing. There it would be milled and made into bread. There would be about seven or eight tons in the wagon, from the local farms around here. Now it tends to be stored for export.

This would have been about twenty-five years ago. There were lots of small slaughterhouses around then, like Baxters, and Broomhalls, which is still going. But now you can't slaughter one on the farm for home consumption. People always used to have pigs killed, and it would then be hung and salted. Everyone had their poultry, their pig, their milk. Now farms are intensified to one degree - either arable, or dairy intensive or beef intensive. There's just not the mixed farms.

Graham Lovell (b. 1960)

Beware of the ram

Although farms in Quedgeley have disappeared under housing, I don't think many farmers have become wealthy because of it. A lot of farmers were tenant farmers anyway, and didn't make any money from the developers. Waterwells Farm has disappeared, and the farmer from Green Farm, who was also a blacksmith and had a real eye for horses, lost his farm. He was a tenant farmer and was loathing the day when his farm was going to be taken from him.

Demolition work underway at the Reformatory. The enormous building dwarfs School Farm, to the left.

School Farm,
Hardwicke,
Gloucester
21. 1. 28

I have great pleasure in testifying to the ability & character of Harry Sims who has managed this farm for me for 5½ years.

He is well able to perform all th manual operations on a mixed farm and is used to the breeding and rearing of cattle, sheep and pigs, both pedigree & non-pedigree and has attended market both for buying & selling.

In milk recording & rationing he has taken the keenest interest.

I have known him nearly all his life & have always found him sober, honest, industrious and in every way reliable to look after m, interests.

Signed: Wm Robinson.

A letter of reference for farmer Harry Sims.

Jack Payne, who had Quedgeley Farm, had a very friendly ram that had been hand-reared. He was very friendly, but you had to make a fuss of him, or he got upset. One day some surveyors arrived with their theodolites to mark out the Quedgeley bypass. They hadn't asked Jack's permission to come on to the land, and they hadn't had the courtesy to introduce themselves. So Jack didn't say anything about the ram. They were working away, and the ram got upset because they hadn't made a fuss of him. So while they were working he gradually moved closer and closer, stopping every few steps to eat some grass, just sneaking up on them. And when he got close enough he knocked them flying. They ran and climbed up some apple trees and were there for quite a while until Jack eventually decided to rescue them.

Another Quedgeley farmer, John Phipps, wrote a book with a solicitor to help farmers who were having legal problems.

Bill Stewart (b. 1940)

A call in the night

As a vet working with farm animals, basic things are just the same – calving cows and treating milk fevers. The diseases haven't changed much and the treatments are perhaps slightly more refined, but the job certainly hasn't changed much. A lot of veterinary practices, though, have given up farm work, partly because it's physically demanding and partly because you never know when you are going to get called out. I still get called out in the middle of the night! In the old days I might come back home with a chicken or a few eggs, but that doesn't happen any more.

Most of the older vets used to practice on their own, so effectively they would be on duty twenty-four hours a day, 365 days a year. When I started you were expected to work hard all week, and work at least every other weekend. Sunday morning was cat spay day!

Bill Stewart (b. 1940)

Work in progress at Alkerton Court Farm in Eastington

Hardwicke Farm.

A giant haystack.

Housing developments have sprung up in the villages on former green field sites, and some on brownfield sites.

Celebration and thanksgiving

From the founding of a church in Hardwicke in the eleventh century it had been under the authority of the parish of Standish. On 1 December 1974 the ecclesiastical parish of Hardwicke came into existence for the first time, it gained 'independence'. In 1999 a service of Holy Communion was conducted by myself, the second Vicar of Hardwicke and current incumbent, in celebration and thanksgiving for the first twenty-five years of the ecclesiastical parish.

Celebration and thanksgiving lay at the heart of the Church's mission and outreach. In celebration people come for baptism and wedding services, in thanksgiving they gather to remember those who have died or mark special moments in their life. There are highlights during the Church's year, the seasons of Advent and Lent giving way to Christmas and Easter, the Feast of St Michael and All Angels, followed by the Feasts of All Souls and All Saints which lead toward the Feast of St Nicholas on 6 December.

Although the Parish church may once have had other 'patrons', for as long as people can remember St Nicholas has watched as Patron Saint over the congregation and people of Hardwicke. A Patron Saint is a saint who, by tradition has been chosen as the special intercessor and advocate of a particular place, person or organization. St Nicholas is a fourth century bishop of Myra, in south-west Turkey, and is most commonly referred to as Santa Claus! As well as these saint's days other important events in the life of the village and nation are marked in the Parish church, the dawning of the Third Millennium, the events of the 11 September 2001, Flower Festivals and the annual observance of Remembrance Sunday.

Although the Parish church of St Nicholas is somewhat remote from the main population of Hardwicke it has and continues to play a central role in the life of the village. Many of its members serve on other village organizations and the village school, the largest Church of England primary school in the Diocese of Gloucester is served by governors, the majority of whom are appointed on the recommendation of the Parochial Church Council. Archbishop William Temple wrote that 'the Church is the only organization that exists for non members', it seeks to serve all who live in the community and even today, in the fast changing years of a new century it still seeks after the ideal and principle to worship God and serve Him through His people.

We serve our neighbours, those who live on the new developments and those who live in the more established housing estates and in the mature houses on the edge of the village by trying to understand their issues and concerns, and then reflecting them in our worship and in our prayers. Of all the feasts and festivals that bring colour to the life of the Church, the service of thanksgiving for the harvest, Harvest Festival, must be among the most popular. Although men and women have given thanks to God for the gifts of creation through each civilization across countless centuries, the Harvest Festival many of us remember with nostalgia is a relatively recently revived feast having its origins with a Cornish priest, R.S. Hawker, who held the first 'modern' Harvest Festival at Morwenstow in 1843.

Traditionally the service was held during the early part of October, at the time of St Luke's Little Summer. (The Feast of St Luke is on 18 October) 'During the early weeks of October the gardens are still a blaze of colour, Michaelmas daisies, deep pink, feathery white, the old-fashioned lavender-coloured and the new blue one are all in bloom still, white marigolds and nasturtiums run riot over the border.' (A quote from *In a Country Parsons Shoes* published 1954 by Pilgrim). The author

One of the estates in Hardwicke built on former farm land.

St Nicholas church at Hardwicke has always had a close relationship with the farming community.

The churchyard at St James church at Quedgeley.

goes on to write 'It is easy to laugh and sneer at the "Feast of St Pumpkin and All Cabbages", but if you are a country priest you must do better than that.' The Harvest Festival, along with Plough Sunday in January, Rogation Sunday in May and Lammas-tide in August are an attempt to make real what the Church has always taught, that life is a partnership between God and His people.

The Harvest Festival still has an important part to play in the life of the Church, but now the traditional elements of the Harvest, the sentimental indulgence of churches stacked with produce from field and garden is balanced by humble 'tin'. Beautiful flowers, fruits and vegetables share the space with tins and packets of food, no less an offering to God but telling an important message, that the Parish church of St Nicholas, which has stood for at least 700 years in its corner of Hardwicke, is not a museum piece - yes it is part of our heritage, but it is also part of our future. And while once the farm workers came to decorate the Lych Gate in thanksgiving for the Harvest, now a new generation come to give thanks, in their own way and for their own generation.

The Revd Thomas Woodhouse

A close community

The farming community is still very close, farmer to farmer. It is a very social community, with skittles teams and so on, just local farmers getting up local teams. There is a real sense of community, with farmers willing to help each other.

Graham Lovell (b. 1960)

The Curtis Hayward tomb in Quedgeley churchyard.

10 Times of Change

Hardwicke's Millennium Stone.

Moving out

We left because our cottage belonged to Curtis Hayward – Curtis Hayward owned all the village then. He wanted to sell – everything was up for sale. We wanted to buy our cottage and it was valued at £600. But Mrs Prout and Mrs Mayo, the farmers, they wanted the cottage for a farm cottage. So when we went to the sale my husband bid our limit, which was £600, but they went on and on and on – they were against each other, they were at loggerheads all the time over everything – at the WI even they were at loggerheads – and it went up to £2,800. Mrs Mayo got it over Mrs Prout. We bought a house at Brockworth after – with water and sanitation.

Marjorie Dobbs
(b. 1916)

Water mains

I can remember them putting the water mains in at Hardwicke when I was at school – that was a big event.

Eric Vick
(b. 1929)

The last party

For many years there was a New Year's Party for the over sixties in Hardwicke Village Hall. There was always a wonderful meal, supplied by Mrs Dawe and her helpers. But the committee themselves became pensioners and none of the younger folk wanted to take it over. So the Millennium Year was the last year the party was held. There's still a lot goes on in the Village Hall – Brownies, short mat bowling, sequence dancing, cricket in the summer and football in the winter.

Betty Brewis
(b. 1922)

A few more houses

I went to school in Cardiff and never thought I would like village life, but I do. This was just fields, it was a lovely friendly community.

It was a gradual change, a few more houses, then the road was put down, then the street lights – we didn't want those. The children used to play in the fields and we would never worry about them. There were cowslips and primroses and bluebells. There wasn't the vandalism there is now.

Bettina Brewis
(b. 1922)

A rural paradise

My memories, as a small child, are that Hardwicke was a rural paradise. The vast housing developments came much later; I recall open fields and unhindered views of the sky, so different to my experience of growing up surrounded by the narrow streets and closely packed houses of inner Gloucester. Whenever I now visit Hardwicke and Quedgeley and ponder the huge developments which have

Gothic Cottage on the Bristol Road, demolished in 1967. 'Highways' was built in its place.

taken place, I cannot help but lament the lost pastoral idyll as it seemed to me as a small child.

Mike Sheridan (now residing in Somerset)

A special house

The first time I saw The Bridge House it was just a tumbledown wreck, a real eye-sore. I couldn't believe that Tony [Green] was really intending to do it up. It was definitely in the sort of state where most people would have knocked it down. Most of the roof had gone and half of one of the pillars was missing from the portico. Tony said it had been fished out of the canal some time earlier. I don't know how long the house had been empty, or when the bridge it originally served had been taken down.

The garden was like a jungle, overgrown with falling down outbuildings all over the place. Tony said local people had told him that the garden once boasted the best display of fruit and vegetables and flowers you have ever seen - funny how quickly nature takes things back. But even in that state there was something very special about the house. Tony was a builder, living in Standish at the time, and he always chose unusual buildings to work on. He liked a challenge. He and his wife Maria planned to renovate The Bridge House and use it for holiday lets. I had worked with Tony on several occasions in the past, installing the lights and electrics in his properties.

Tony and Maria and the team worked hard on the house for six months, lovingly restoring it. The broken pillar was repaired and restored to its proper position. I think everyone felt they were rescuing a little piece of history. By the time the house was finished, no-one really wanted it tso be a holiday cottage; I think everyone felt it deserved

Hardwicke Bridge House was in a sorry of state when renovation work began in 1993.

A view of the back of Hardwicke Bridge House.

more of a commitment than that. I certainly did. My wife was adamant that she didn't want to move from Stroud, but I eventually persuaded her to come and look at the Bridge House. It was a beautiful day in late July and in the sunshine the house looked fantastic. My wife was smitten – it was definitely a case of love at first sight. We moved in that September with our two young daughters – but friends and family thought we would never make it through that first, muddy winter. But we did. Nine years and another daughter later, we're still here!

Tony died unexpectedly and very suddenly just after Christmas 2000. The Bridge House is just part of the amazing legacy of restored buildings that he left behind.

Matt Ashenford
(b. 1963)

Open countryside

We had no car, so the whole family would cycle to Hardwicke from Gloucester, a journey of about six miles. By the time half the journey had been completed, we would be in open countryside – Gloucester has grown since those days!

Mike Sheridan

'No' to the street lights

It's a very different village now – it's almost like urban Hardwicke and rural Hardwicke. I used to know everybody in the village. We welcomed a few houses in the early days, but Miss Olive Lloyd-Baker was adamant we didn't want street lighting, or even pavements round here. I was on the parish council for many years and we were dead against it – the parish council was unanimous on that.

Eric Vick
(b. 1929)

Hardwicke Bridge House, restored to its former glory.

Puddleducks Nursery – this building may at one time have been a vicarage.

Watching the changes

I was brought up in Hildyard Close in the late 1960s, early 1970s and went to Quedgeley primary school in School Lane – where Quedgeley Community Centre now is. My grandparents lived in Naas Lane, Quedgeley and my grandfather was an MOD fireman at RAF Quedgeley. I used to play with friends from Springfield in the fields between Elmgrove Road East and Sellars Road, which was known as the Ashpath. We sometimes played in the half-built houses at the bottom of Hildyard Close – probably even the one we are living in now! As a short cut to the Bristol Road we would cut across the field at the bottom of Hildyard Close, which is now Lower Meadow. Often we would cross the fields the other side of Springfield to reach a huge mound of earth where Overbrook Road is now. From here we could see the old

BP station and Sunnyfield Road, where I later lived.

I can remember watching the fields around being turned into the Elmgrove housing estate and the building of the 'new' Morning Star pub – the old one stood next to where the current one is now situated. An even more vivid memory is seeing Hardwicke Post Office on fire after it was struck by lightening. Sometimes I would go fishing in the canal with my sister's boyfriend and we would get talking to the old bridgekeeper, Mr Prosser, who was later a neighbour at Sunnyfield Road. I can also remember cycling along the canal towpath from Pilot Bridge down to the old Hardwicke bridge – which has now gone – and across to Hardwicke church. We used to mess around in the churchyard – later I was employed by Revd Stickland to paint the inside of the church. We would

The Queen's Golden Jubilee was celebrated with a street party by local residents.

also play in and around Fieldcourt House, which was opposite Fieldcourt school, but which has since been demolished. I used to walk my girlfriend Jayne – now my wife - home down the Bristol Road before Tesco was built.

We now live in Hildyard Close – in a house formerly owned by the family of an old school friend. Many of my former school friends still live around here, which was one of the reasons the recent street party to celebrate the Queen's Gold Jubilee was such a special event.

Nick Bailey

Walking on velvet

One thing I miss today is the open fields. Where we live today (on the Bristol Road), there were just two houses between us and the canal – Fieldcourt Farmhouse and the Gardener's Cottage, which stood at the far corner of what became Severn Vale school's playing field. The school was built in 1962. Behind our house we had large orchards. In wintertime we would walk between the trees, the moss below our feet – it was like walking on velvet – and the birds would be singing in the treetops. All that came to an end in 1974 when the developers moved in and the Field Court development began. I remember the large bulldozer ploughing through the orchards and recklessly pushing them all down. I cried that day! I remember it was the nesting season and all the poor birds, their treetops lost, flying round and around, not knowing where to go.

Richard Cale
(b. 1943)

Hardwicke's history

Just like any other place Hardwicke has a history and in 1995 the committee of the village magazine, *Hardwicke Matters*, decided to try and start a local history group. We booked the Gloucestershire historian, Bryan Jerrard, to give a talk, 'Hardwicke's History', at the village hall and used that occasion to invite members to join the history group.

We were soon to discover that Hardwicke's history was often fairly well hidden. Oh, there was the Victoria History entry, but that left much out and often posed more questions than it gave answers to. We were to discover that there was enough material in the researchers' notes that was *not* published to keep us going for a lifetime.

One family decided to investigate Hardwicke's part in the Civil War. Despite the close proximity of Gloucester, and its famous battle, it seems Hardwicke was a quiet place during the war. Famous in those days for its cheese and cider it was left in peace, presumably so both sides could benefit from its produce in their turn of being in charge of the area! Like many other locations there is a story that Oliver Cromwell once stayed in one of the village's oldest buildings, the Old Hall. Otherwise nothing at all of note seems to have happened.

Another member took on the task of documenting the history of the Hardwicke Reformatory, reputedly the world's first 'Approved School', and which became world famous in its time. After decades of being allowed to fall into disrepair the building has finally been demolished, and a piece of local and national history has been lost. There have been many other histories of this institution, some recording facts others had missed. The main task became one of collating all the pieces into a coherent whole. There was some new information regarding the uses of the building after the Reformatory had closed.

Whilst looking into the history of the local

Celebrating the Queen's Golden Jubilee.

Community spirit lives on as the Golden Jubilee celebrations demonstrate.

squire's estate one member was annoyed to read that an area called 'Beaurepair' in medieval times, along with a waterway of the same name, had been 'lost'. A few months research enabled us to make a case to the authorities that the unnamed brook forming the southern boundary of the parish was the long lost Beaurepair waterway. It will now appear as such on future Ordnance Survey maps. A small victory and one more piece of the village history reclaimed. Another story was supposed to explain the name of Madam's End Farm, another of the village's ancient buildings. The farm lies on what may have once been the King's Highway to Bristol. Henry VIII, in procession from Bristol to Gloucester, was reputed to have stayed there when his then wife refused to go any further that day. It was certainly the end of that day's journey for 'Madam', but did it have greater implications?

The full story of Amer Butler, the local squire

in the fourteenth century, is not known, but he seems to have been a nasty piece. He was put in front of the King's magistrates for wife beating, wrongful imprisonment, maintaining felons, not repairing a local bridge, blocking the local water supply (Beaurepair Brook) to fill his fishing lake and sundry other charges. It may have been a family trait as apparently his brother was no better!

Most of the 'official' history of Hardwicke is documented in the County Record Office but there is still work to do on the day-to-day events and the recording of the lives of ordinary people. Though, unfortunately, the society has became dormant, as membership dwindled, one activity still goes on spasmodically, the recording of living history, the memories of the older residents of the village. The recording of local history, and particularly living history, is a very important thing for the future. The big events always have their historians, but the common people are only bit players in the big scene. We may often chuckle at the values and way of life of our parents and grandparents, but it is those things that have contributed to forming much of the world we live in now. Times are changing though, the world is getting smaller through easy travel and the Internet and we are taking on values, fashions and habits from further away every year. Also of importance is the preservation of documents, even mundane shopping bills will be of interest to future historians, and photos, even family pictures, are valid historical documents. We have found that it is most often modesty that has prevented people coming forward rather than a need for privacy. In the past things hardly changed, for a hundred years at a time, then a few decades became the unit of 'progress'; now the world seems to change significantly from year to year. What happened in the life of Mr and Mrs Everyman in the last hundred years provides clues to the state of our present world and the recording of those times is very important.

Hopefully interest in local history in Hardwicke will wax again at some time in the future, so the files are being kept safely for that time. An account similar to this could probably be written for hundreds of small communities. Some are lucky and interest is maintained until the book, which is usually the aim, detailing the whole local history is written. Hardwicke's turn will come one day, I am sure of that.

Dave Bailes

Northern lights

One night I went to visit Valerie when she was living at Beryl's Close. I was just leaving there, it must have been about midnight and the car was white – it was really cold. You don't get many nights like that now. I turned

Fun for all ages at the Jubilee celebrations.

Hardwicke Bridge House viewed from Stank Lane.

round and looked towards the north and there were all these dancing lights in the sky. It was the Aurora Borealis – the Northern Lights. I called Valerie's dad out to see them, and he said in all his years he had never seen anything like that. You won't see it now because of all the modern lighting – you need the darkness of the countryside to see it. It was a spectacular show.

Nick Hodges

A village magazine

Back in 1987 a piece of buff coloured paper, typed on both sides and photocopied, with the title *Hardwicke Matters* dropped onto the doormats of every house in Hardwicke. The first paragraph started: 'If your first thought is "Not more bumph through the door", don't give up just yet'. That was the first issue of a parish newsletter that is now in its fifteenth successful year of publication. Too successful if the backlog of advertisers waiting for their turn is anything to judge by. *Hardwicke Matters* has been used as an example of how to organise a village magazine and the editor was once drafted in to give a talk on starting a magazine. That first, double-sided single photocopied sheet was the parish council's response to a perceived need for a way to get village news promulgated. They formed a committee from residents and one of those original members is still serving on the present committee and one more who started soon after issue one. Items from that first issue included a complaint about low flying military aircraft (no change there then), a suggestion that Neighbourhood Watch Schemes be started in Hardwicke (no change there again) and that the Boundary Commission is still considering whether Hardwicke should be in Stroud District or Gloucester (still being pondered every now and again!). The last entry on the back was a competition, for a name for the newsletter. I don't know if there were any entries, but it has stayed *Hardwicke Matters*, with its possibly intended double meaning, ever since. It was published intermittently, still as a single sheet, until 1989 when Tom Sullivan, a partner in the village store cum post office, took over as editor. It went 'independent' and had grown to sixteen pages soon after and was beginning to pay for itself with adverts for local companies. By the time it had grown to thirty-two plus pages it made a small profit, and still does. A portion of this profit is put back into the village as donations to organisations. During this time a small army of deliverers was established to ensure every home got its copy.

I joined the committee as assistant editor in 1992 and took over as editor in 1993. In those days, before the time of the now almost ubiquitous PC, we used a slow old Amstrad 8256 computer, little more than a glorified typewriter. Printing out the copy took most of an evening, and then it had to be cut into pieces and pasted back together to make full pages. The adverts had to be glued in as well, there was no software to produce print ready pages with pictures easily available then.

I relinquished the editorship in 1999, due to ill health, to our then treasurer, Phil Mountjoy, who took good care of it until 2001 when our present editor, Sandra Ashenford, took over. Each editor stamps their own influence on the appearance of the magazine, and this helps to prevent it from getting too staid or stodgy. The fact that *Hardwicke Matters* has lasted for fifteen very successful years is owed to the dedication shown by the members of the committee. Without that long term loyalty it would not have been so easy to keep going. Not to be forgotten are the many villagers who have turned out once a month, in all weathers, to get the *Hardwicke Matters* through every letter-box in the village; to all the surgeries, schools, shops, hairdressers and library. Unless a magazine actually gets to its readers it is a bit of a failure. Once a year we invite them all to have a couple of drinks with us, something to eat and maybe a game of skittles – one day they will terrify us by everyone accepting the invitation! Through their efforts 1,850 copies find their way home every month.

Also needing mention are the many correspondents from village organisations, schools, the churches etc, the letter writers and all those who have contributed the articles that make the magazine *Hardwicke Matters*.

Dave Bailes

The Ashenford family by the gate of Hardwicke Bridge House, where bridgeman Tom Fredericks once cut hair and sold flowers.